Christian Churches
in the United States

An Illustrated History of the Church

Christianity in the New World/from 1500 to 1800
By Martin E. Marty

Christian Churches in the United States/from 1800
By Martin E. Marty

An index for these two volumes is included
in *Christian Churches in the United States*.

The complete Illustrated History of the Church *series also includes the ten books listed below:*

The First Christians
From the beginnings to A.D. 180

The Church Established
180-381

The End of the Ancient World
381-630

The Formation of Christian Europe
600-900

The Middle Ages
900-1300

**The Church
in the Age of Humanism**
1300-1500

Protestant and Catholic Reform
1500-1700

The Church in Revolutionary Times
1700-1850

The Church and the Modern Nations
1850-1920

The Church Today
1920-1981

Christian Churches in the United States

Martin E. Marty

Fairfax M. Cone Distinguished Service Professor
of the History of Modern Christianity, the University of Chicago

Illustrated by Reg Sandland

Book design: Reg Sandland

Library of Congress Catalog Card Number: 86-45818

ISBN: 0-06-065435-X

The following books in *An Illustrated History of the
Church series,* published by Harper & Row, Publishers,
Inc., were created and produced by Editoriale Jaca Book:
*The First Christians; The Church Established; The End of
the Ancient World; The Formation of Christian Europe;
The Middle Ages; The Church in the Age of Humanism;
Protestant and Catholic Reform; The Church in Revolution-
ary Times; The Church and the Modern Nations; The
Church Today.*

87 88 89 90 91 10 9 8 7 6 5 4 3 2 1

Table of Contents

5

Introduction

American church history is different from other church history. The reader of church history has an easy time of it when dealing with the ancient Church. Most of the traces it left are lost. The monuments have crumbled, the books are dust. What is left are a few hundred or thousand pages of comment on Christian life, comment which only hints at how diverse church ways must have been.

Even in the Middle Ages, it is not hard to follow the plot of the story. There were two churches, Eastern and Western. The Western church, under the Roman pope, united the people of Europe. Telling the story of Roman Catholicism took care of almost everything that mattered to people of Western culture.

The third big chapter in most people's books deals with Catholic and Protestant Reformation in the 1500s. Now the plot begins to get confused. Still, one can follow the story line fairly easily because in almost every nation there was one privileged or majority faith—Catholic, Anglican, Lutheran, or Reformed—with usually one or more minority churches to make the story interesting.

When we come to the fourth section, with which this book deals, something new has happened. About two centuries ago, people for the first time experienced "religious freedom," or "the separation of church and state." The big change came at the time of the birth of the United States, and America was the scene of much of the action.

Religious freedom meant that all kinds of religious groups would live together on equal terms. Immigrants brought their many and varied churches to America with them. Moreover, in America persons were free to start new

1800

churches to attract other people. Now we must keep track of hundreds of church bodies. How can we do that and still keep the story of the twenty-century-old Church alive and moving?

It doesn't work simply to say "in 1798 this happened" and "in 1799 this happened and then, and then, and then...." Nor can we make the history come alive by running through an alphabet of churches: Adventist, Baptist, Congregational, Disciples, Episcopalian, Friends, and so on.

Instead, we begin many chapters by visiting a typical church of some denomination or other in a typical city. We ask: "What are they doing? Why are they doing it? Why are they here? Where did they come from?"

To answer such questions, we tell the story of an important person who has a vision—a strong grasp of the special purpose—for this religious group, this part of the Church. What was important to this person? What did he or she hope would happen to those who shared the vision? How did the vision turn out? In most cases, we will follow the vision in the life of that church or religious group, bringing the story to the present time.

Sometimes churches act together—for example, when they want to help migrant workers, or serve a cause of peace. So part of the time we shall talk about interchurch agencies or trends. Most of the time, however, this history of the *Church* in America will keep on telling the story of the *churches*. As such, this book will present the latest unfolding of the story that began with Jesus twenty centuries ago.

As an historian, I look backward, but as a believer, I look ahead. Christians believe that as long as the world survives, the story of the Church will continue. Jesus promised this. So to symbolize this belief, this promise, I have chosen to dedicate this book to a grandson. He has a chance, along with readers of this book who are much younger than the author, to help *make* history—so that someone can write about the Church in the twenty-first century.

—Martin E. Marty

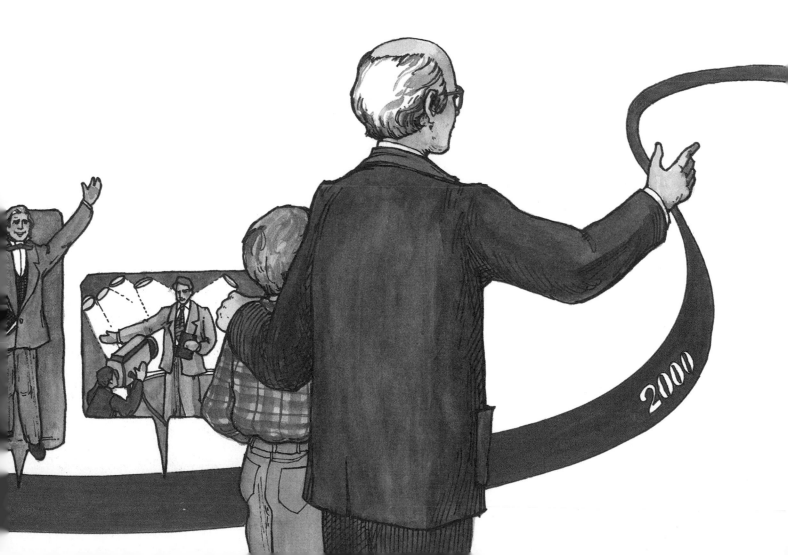

I
Telling the Story of the Churches in the United States

1 Why Are There So Many Churches? Denominationalism

People who came to America from Europe brought many styles of Christianity. Freedom of religion in America allowed denominations to compete with each other. Also, many new church bodies started.

Almost all Christians agree that Jesus Christ wanted his followers to live in unity with each other. The New Testament writings about the Church say that it should be one, just as there is "one Lord, one faith, one baptism, one God and father of all . . ."

Despite the belief that the Christian Church is and should be one, America has many church bodies, which we usually call denominations. One glance at the Yellow Pages in the phone book of any medium-sized city will show how many different ones there are. *A Yearbook of American and Canadian Churches* lists well over 200 bodies. Other reference works list even more.

How did there come to be so many different and often competing churches? The answer to that question goes back far before the founding of America. The earliest Christians did not live in perfect harmony by any means. A thousand years after Christ, the European Church split into Eastern and Western branches, the families that today we usually call Orthodox and Roman Catholic. The members of each belonged to different parts of the Roman Empire. They argued over some points of doctrine. For almost a thousand years they have gone their separate ways. The two developed different ways of worship. Today a few million Americans are heirs of Orthodoxy, while fifty million are Roman Catholic, making up the largest church body in America.

The small churches which grew up before 1500 were not allowed a free life. Waldensians, Albigensians, Hussites, Cathari—most of their names are forgotten today—had to hide in mountain villages, or they were snuffed out. Only the Moravians, who were heirs of the Hussites, sent many offspring to America.

American denominations result largely from the Protestant Reformation of the 1500s. All over Europe separate reform movements sprang up, and all resisted the kind of unity represented by the pope in the Roman Catholic Church. The Reformation was a kind of "spontaneous combustion" or a "contagion" of church movements. Leaders argued with each other. Separate churches grew up in the different regions and territories or nations.

Each of these European nations sent emigrants to America. They brought with them their separate and divided styles of Christianity. Lutherans who came from Norway, Sweden, Denmark, Finland, and Germany lived in separate national groups in America and did not speak each other's languages or know each other's ways. Emigrants from each country had one or more church bodies of their own in America.

The time period of an emigrant's arrival in America made a difference also. The Lutherans who arrived before 1776 became more like other American Protestants. Most of those who arrived in the 1800s were more standoffish, mistrustful not only of other American Christians but also of each other. So at one time there were dozens of Lutheran church bodies in America.

Sometimes churches divided because of social issues. For example, just before or during the Civil War, southern churches insisted on their right to allow members to hold slaves. Soon there were separate Methodist, Baptist, and Presbyterian churches in the South and North.

Churches also divided over various doctrines and practices. For instance, at one time Presbyterians who favored revivals were split from those who opposed them. Some Congregationalists argued about the age at which people should be baptized and the manner of baptism. Those who wanted baptism for adults only and baptism by immersion became Baptists.

Some new bodies developed through the ideas of individual people. Joseph Smith founded the Mormons, Mary Baker Eddy had the vision that launched Christian Science, and William Miller and Ellen Gould White helped give birth to Adventism.

Denominationalism has worked well in America. It is a sign of freedom: People can join existing churches, take part in splitting them, or help invent new ones. The state cannot interfere, and other Christians must stand by and let the new denomination make its way.

Denominations compete. They also assure to their members the freedom to think they are holding on to the truth while others may be straying. Denominationalism allows people choice. Yet it also forces Christians to find ways to overcome division and show that they are still somehow one in Christ. ●

This map shows some of the groups of people who came to America from Europe and Africa.

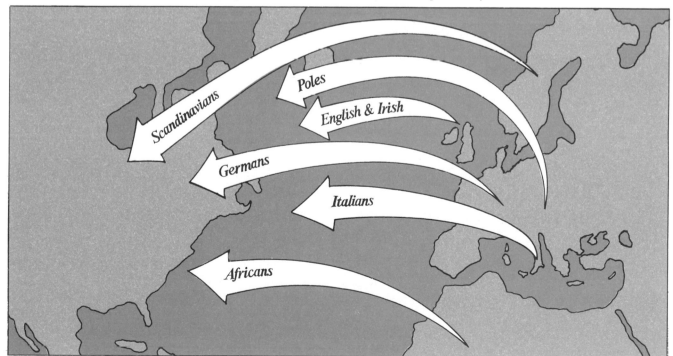

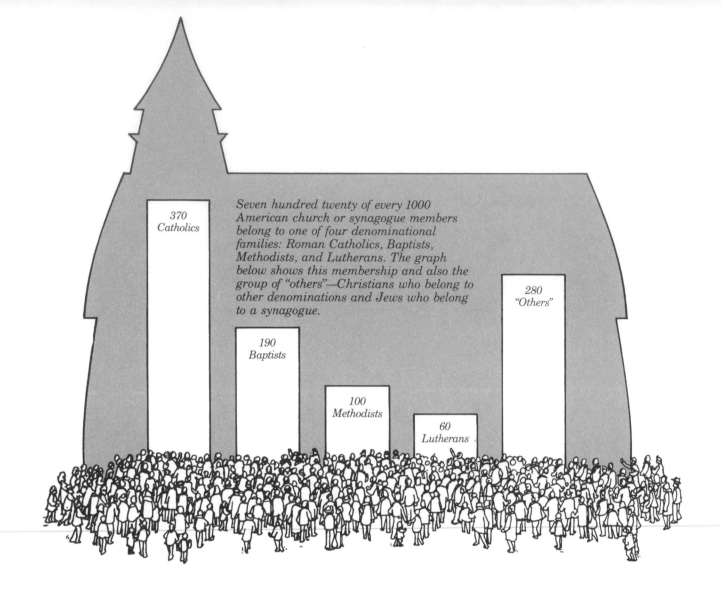

Seven hundred twenty of every 1000 American church or synagogue members belong to one of four denominational families: Roman Catholics, Baptists, Methodists, and Lutherans. The graph below shows this membership and also the group of "others"—Christians who belong to other denominations and Jews who belong to a synagogue.

370 Catholics

190 Baptists

100 Methodists

60 Lutherans

280 "Others"

2 How Are the Many Churches One? Christian Unity

Christians are not as divided as they appear. Most American denominations are in one of a few large "church families." And there is a strong movement toward unity and working together among American churches.

Are Americans as divided as the church signs in each city or the many listings in the Yellow Pages suggest? No. American churches come in families. While families have feuds and fights, they are still families, and they have much in common. In a small town with 1,000 church members—if the town were a perfect miniature of the nation—eleven of these families would together claim all but 87 of these 1,000 believers. There would be 370 Roman Catholics, 190 Baptists, 100 Methodists, and 60 Lutherans. In other words, 720 of the 1,000 would be in four families. There would be 46 Jews, who are not a part of the problem of Christian unity. Next to them would be 37 in Christian (like the Disciples of Christ) churches, 31 Presbyterians, 26 Eastern Orthodox, 23 Episcopalians, 17 Mormons, and 13 members of the United Church of Christ.

Of course, there are several kinds of Methodists and Lutherans, and many kinds of Christians in the "others" category, but Americans are not as confused by competing claims as one might think. While free to switch denominations, six out of ten American church members live their whole lives in the same one.

Within their own churches, however, many work for unity. In a typical city most of the more established congregations band together for cooperative work in a church council or federation. The members have not settled all of their differences. They often worship together or have joint activities in the community. There are state councils, and the National Council of Churches includes most of the mainline Protestant and Orthodox churches and has friendly relations with Roman Catholics.

Mergers also facilitate unity. These usually come about because people in a family are tired of feuding or being separate. The Lutherans, who once had dozens of different church bodies, are moving toward one large united body, alongside one rather large separate denomination and a few tiny splinters. Methodists north and south reunited in 1939. Most traditions can point to such movements, such tidying up of their separate houses.

Most mergers have been among people of a single Protestant family who were divided because they came over from different European nations, or arrived at different times, or split over an issue when they got here. There is one dramatic exception. In 1957 the Evangelical and Reformed Church and the Congregational Church came together to form the United Church of Christ. The ancestors of members were, on the Congregational side, largely from England. On the Evangelical and Reformed side, they were mostly from Germany. Some Congregationalists stayed out of the union, so that after the merger there still are two denominations; but the trend was clear.

The efforts to create a better spirit of Christian unity have produced great changes. Christians have cut competition and increased cooperation. They often pray together. They are less disturbed than they once were by "mixed marriages"—marriages of persons from different ethnic or religious groups—which once split families. While remaining in separate churches, they have learned to accept each other's ministries. Many of them rejoice when other churches prosper and mourn when they suffer hard times. Even the conservative Protestants who once opposed the church unity movement have formed many such movements of their own. Sometimes the moderately liberal and the moderately conservative groups work together.

No one pretends that America has overcome the "scandal" of Christian disunity. Most believers, however, believe they are on the way to finding a balance. They want to cherish and enjoy their own traditions and the specific truths they have come to know in their own groups. At the same time, they want to share the burdens and joys of others who are also called by Christ. The movement toward Christian unity may have slowed in recent years, but the spirit of concord is very much alive.

As different persons share a family name and are a family, different Christian groups are usually parts of denominational families.

3 The Map of Religious Groups

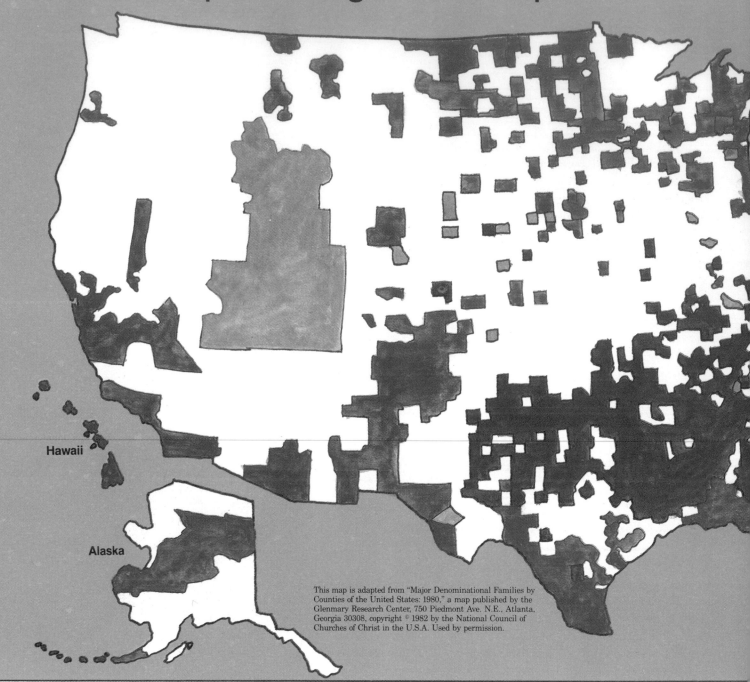

Hawaii

Alaska

This map is adapted from "Major Denominational Families by Counties of the United States: 1980," a map published by the Glenmary Research Center, 750 Piedmont Ave. N.E., Atlanta, Georgia 30308, copyright © 1982 by the National Council of Churches of Christ in the U.S.A. Used by permission.

As the map on these pages shows, most American church bodies are concentrated in particular regions. Catholics, Baptists, Methodists, Lutherans, and Mormons are each dominant in large areas.

Americans like to call theirs a "pluralist society." By this they mean that many religions are represented, and that they are all equally protected by law. But after two centuries of national life and almost five centuries after the discovery of the hemisphere by Europeans, American religion is still regionalized. Almost everywhere one denominational family tends to dominate over the others. So far as a religious map is concerned we might speak of the "five nations of America."

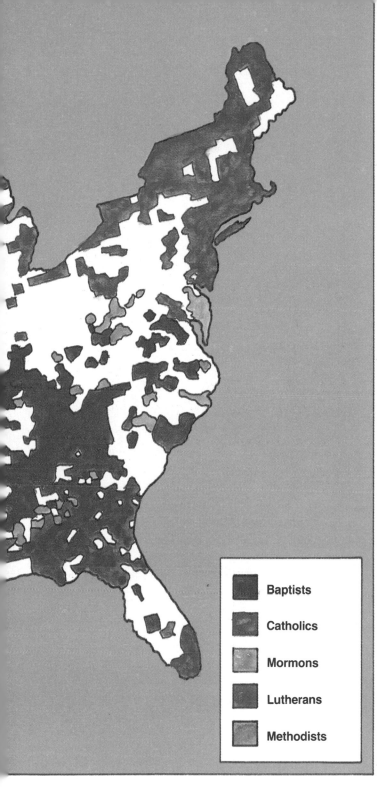

The colored areas on this map show counties in the United States where more than half of all church members belong to one particular denominational family. Five church families dominate; they are Baptists, Catholics, Mormons, Lutherans, Methodists. The map is explained in the text, beginning on page fourteen, directly under the map.

Baptists

Catholics

Mormons

Lutherans

Methodists

In a typical county, sixty percent of the people are members of some church. We are using a map to show the religious preference of Americans by county. If more than half the church members in a county are from one group, the mapmaker has shown the county in a solid color representing that denomination. Many counties are white. This does not mean that those counties have fewer church or synagogue members than other counties. Rather, it shows that no one denominational family dominates. If we were also to show

the counties where one group has the loyalty of at least twenty-five percent of church members, not many counties would remain uncolored, but the map would have to show quite a few additional denominations.

First, starting from the bottom, is the Baptist South. Next, above them, in what we may call the "south of the North and the north of the South" is Methodist America. The third section of religious America is the upper Midwest, where there is a Lutheran sweep. Fourth is the Mormon kingdom. In the rest of America, Roman Catholics are the most dominant group. In most urban areas, many religious groups are large, but Roman Catholicism dominates.

Whoever knows the history of American religion might well wonder where the colonial "big three"—the Episcopalians, Congregationalists, and Presbyterians—survive. The late colonial leaders foresaw an America in which these three churches would move straight west, dividing the territory among themselves. These leaders would be surprised by today's map.

How did the denominations which predominated in early America come to be outnumbered? First, these churches were English-speaking. After 1776, fewer immigrants came from England. The non-English-speaking newcomers were more likely to be Catholics, Lutherans, or Jews. To this day, Jews and Catholics are concentrated in urban America. Second, the oldline groups were not successful in winning the blacks, as Methodists and Baptists were in both the rural South and the urban North. Third, the three oldline denominations were less successful as revivalists, so they lost out to Methodists and Baptists in the white South and elsewhere.

This means that the principal denominations of colonial America are now thinly spread everywhere, exerting quiet influence. Yet almost nowhere do they dominate enough to determine the culture. Leaving a strong stamp on the culture is the task or privilege of Catholics, Baptists, Methodists, Lutherans, and Mormons.

4 The Main Events of United States Church History

Important events in American history have influenced the life of the churches. Among them are immigration, the movement westward, the growth of cities and industry, and many different groups living side by side.

As we observe the individual denominations, it is important to know the main plot of the history of the nation and its churches. What happened in the larger national environment? Several main themes stand out.

1. *Nation-building.* In more cases than not, the churches and church people played a part on the side of the patriots, supporting the War for Independence. They favored the new Constitution. Many churches had been supported by law and tax in colonial days, and now they had to learn how to be on their own. They invented competitive denominations, asked for voluntary support, and prospered.

2. *Revivalism and the Frontier.* Religion moved west across the mountains in the second generation of United States life, after 1800. It moved in a special way. Leaders noticed that while people may once have feared God, they had to be fired up anew to build churches and be moral. So leaders invented a language that appealed to people on the frontier. They spoke in emotional terms of how bad life was without God and how great conversion and loyalty were. People came to camp meetings and revivals, outdoors and in. Frontier people responded. They came together in churches. It appears that Catholics used similar techniques to gain and keep the loyalty of new immigrants in the cities.

3. *The Protestant Empire.* Between the revival era which began around 1801-02, and the Civil War (1861-1865), while Protestants still had much of the nation to themselves, they built up a kind of empire. They did not have state or legal support. But they did get people to support voluntarily a network of organizations. The members got together to send missionaries to the frontier or overseas. They published and distributed tracts, started Sunday schools, and distributed Bibles. Some worked for reform by opposing alcoholic beverages, dueling, prostitution, and eventually slavery. Protestant Christians wanted to have the nation to themselves, so they made life unattractive and sometimes miserable for Catholics, who after 1840 were coming in much greater numbers.

4. *Division into North and South.* Most members of a given church, whether from the North or the South, held to the same creeds. Yet from the 1840s through the Civil War, the "big three" churches—Baptist, Methodist, and Presbyterian—divided. In the South, church leaders said that the Bible allowed for slavery and that slavery was a moral system. In the North, most leaders said that the institution of slavery was wrong and had to be abolished. Long after the war, America tended to have two warring styles of being religious, with the South always more resistant to change.

5. *Immigration.* America was always a nation of immigrants, from the time 10,000 years ago and more when Asians crossed to Alaska to become the "Indians." Yet in the Protestant empire "immigration" first meant the arrival of non-English-speaking Protestants from the European continent. They brought different ways. They were more likely to drink alcohol or use Sunday for boisterous recreation than were the more staid settlers from England. More troubling to some was the later immigration of non-Protestants—Catholics from Ireland and Germany and later from southern and eastern Europe, Orthodox Christians from the East, Jews, and on the West Coast, Orientals. The Statue of Liberty welcomed them, but newcomers did seem to threaten those who wanted a Protestant nation. In effect, America said, "You can come, but you must change." Religion had much to do with their changing. The churches of America took care of immigrants. They tried to convert some and educate or give relief to many. Jews who had arrived earlier eventually helped welcome newer Jews, and the old Catholic population helped the newer one to feel at home in America.

6. *Industrialization and Urbanization.* The building of factories and of manufacturing cities may not sound like an event in church history, but it had great importance for the churches. In the late 1800s, people who for centuries had been farmers or town dwellers were uprooted to form cities of millions. Churches had to find new strategies for reaching out to such crowds. People were lonely, they were victims of injustice, they were tempted to new sins. The churches ministered to them.

The United States has always been a nation of immigrants. The first immigrants came as settlers from Europe or as slaves from Africa. Since 1975, many people have come from Asian countries, such as Vietnam and Laos. Pictured in this 1979 photo are Vietnamese refugees in Hong Kong, awaiting a move to permanent homes.

7. *The Era of Pluralism.* Even in the 1970s and 1980s America kept on welcoming new sets of people, including "boat people" from Vietnam, Cubans and Haitians from the southeast, and Hispanics from the southwest. Sometimes the welcome was grudging. Still, new peoples found a home in the American mix. They always added color to the mix. Gone were the days of the 1800s when Protestantism or a simple "civil religion" held the nation together. In the 1970s and 1980s people had to bend and stretch their old practices to make room for Eastern "cults" which frightened them. They resented the fact that, because people did not agree on matters of faith,

they could no longer take for granted prayer in school or public places. Citizens had to find new ways to be tolerant of each other and civil to each other. The Christian ecumenical movement and interfaith organizations helped in the course. Americans busied themselves trying to be one nation of many faiths. The terms of that life seemed to change from year to year. The churches did what they could to understand the change, to support what they agreed with, and to resist what they had to. But all kept on learning that America is a land of great religious diversity and that diversity was a challenge.

17

5 Separation of Church and State

Churches in America are not supported by the government; instead, they pay their own expenses. This was a new idea to most people in 1776, but now it is taken for granted by most Americans.
This separation of church and state has led American Christians to support strongly the pastors and churches they have chosen.

Whether churches in America want to compete or cooperate, stay apart or get together, they are free to make their own decisions. In most cases the lay members, not only the clergy, take part in the decisions.

What is remarkable about this freedom is that the United States government is not involved in the choices churches make. Americans take this so much for granted that they have a hard time picturing that the American separation of church and state is a late arrival in history and even today is a rarity in the world. In most European nations something still remains of an "established church." Some church funds there come from tax monies. There may be something on the order of a "Department of Church Affairs" in the government. While church establishment by law is less powerful there now than it once was, the state still usually determines the life of the church to some extent.

Beyond the bounds of Christianity, in the other major religions of the world, "church" and state are also sometimes united. In Iran, the ayatollahs, leaders of the clergy, see to it that church and state are somehow united. In Israel, Orthodox Judaism has privileges denied to other groups by law. In some parts of Asia, Buddhism or Hinduism gains state support, and other groups are restricted.

The European immigrants before 1776 did not plan to develop a new pattern on the American shores. They were used to state-supported religion and expected to continue it. But sooner or later, they learned that they could have healthier and happier colonies if the government took away tax support of the churches, removed legal privilege, and "tolerated" other churches.

In the course of time in each colony, and later in each state, the idea of merely tolerating minority churches was not enough. All the churches insisted on equal rights. All citizens could be free to belong to any church or to no church, without either gaining or losing legal rights or social position. Leaders like Thomas Jefferson and James Madison in Virginia argued that religion was a matter of "opinion." You cannot, they said, force opinions on someone else. To ask citizens to support or "believe in" a church that they did not agree with was to make liars or prisoners out of them.

Rather than subsidize or give privilege to one church, many churches, or even all churches, national and state constitutions written after the Revolutionary War "disestablished" the churches. Americans say that they thus "separate church and state." The state owed the church protection but not privilege. Christian groups had the same rights as other groups to express themselves.

Christian clergy sometimes worked to create this separation. Baptists and Quakers were among the leaders who allied with Jefferson and Madison. Other Christians resisted the change. People wondered how morality could be upheld if the state did not subsidize and promote religion. Would the churches not become empty, and fall into disrepair?

One of the leaders in New England, the Reverend Lyman Beecher (1775-1863), worked hard to keep a privileged Congregational church in Connecticut. When in 1819, long after the writing of the United States Constitution, the Connecticut legislature and the people voted to break the bond between church and state, the Reverend Mr. Beecher fell into the deepest gloom. His children remembered him sitting in a cane-backed chair, mourning what could be the darkest day for religion. Soon after, however, he was running around saying that separation was "the best thing that ever happened for religion" in the state of Connecticut.

Cutting the tie meant that churches were henceforth on their own. They had to compete for members. Ministers had to preach in a lively way to get people to support the churches. People did not resent the clergy the way they did in countries where the pastors were like government employees. People were free to pick the minister or congregation of their choice. If one style did not please them, they could find another. If no style pleased them, they could invent another. Churches grew and were supported as never before.

Public opinion polls have asked questions about people's belief in God and in life after death. America appears, at least to poll takers, to have a much higher percentage of believers than do the nations of traditionally Christian Europe. These comparative figures are not used to boast about how good Americans are, but to give evidence that religion without the support of the state has done better than either admirers or critics two centuries ago thought it could do.

Separating church and state did not mean that the nation was hostile to the churches. Legislatures have allowed church property to remain free of taxation, an important benefit to the churches. There are chaplains in the legislatures, a sign of friendliness to religion. Often there are legal arguments when the state believes that the churches are wrong, for example, when they refuse to pay taxes on property which they do not use for religious purposes. Sometimes churches feel crowded and claim that the state cramps religion, for example, by limiting prayer in public schools. For the most part, however, the system has worked. Americans applaud it. ●

Connecticut Congregationalist Lyman Beecher was depressed when state support for his denomination ended in 1819.

19

6 The Nation in Miniature: A City of Church

In Typical City, U.S.A., described in this chapter, each major church family has a single congregation. We will visit each church and learn something of its history and its life today.

It is difficult to tell the story of the Christian Church in America. How can a person keep in mind "the Church" when there are hundreds of "churches," or church bodies? To make sense of it all, we must cluster the many denominations into families and then make our way among the families.

This book begins to provide a plot by presenting the whole United States as a single middle-sized city. Each church body has a single building and congregation in that symbolic city. In Typical City, the location of church buildings reflects when the groups started. The location may also tell us about the social classes most typical of each church body.

We shall, for most groups, look backward to observe a person who had a vision for that church body and its place in American life.

First of all, downtown in Typical City are the churches which we can trace back to colonial American days: the Roman Catholic Church, symbolically on the east side of town, and then, south of it, the Episcopal Church. To the north of downtown are the Congregational Church (United Church of Christ) and its liberal offspring from old New England, the Unitarian Universalist Association, as it is today called. Between them is the Presbyterian Church. We can call these five the "oldline" churches. They dominated America before 1800. Near them, at the edge of downtown, are heirs of two colonial "outsider" churches, the Baptists and the Quakers.

Since Typical City is a miniature of the United States, the west side symbolizes the frontier. On the southwest side are four churches representing bodies which grew rapidly while white Americans were settling the territory west of the original colonies on the coast. First are the Methodists and the Southern Baptists, both of whom outstripped the oldline churches and by 1800 became the two largest Protestant groups. Then near them are two which wanted to restore the primitive Gospel on the frontier or to reveal "latter-day saints." These are the Disciples of Christ and the Mormons, both of which originated in America in the first half of the 1800s. We will call these four bodies "heirs of the frontier."

At the time such bodies were developing, black churches were growing. While there are scores of church bodies, most fall into the families of black Baptists and Methodists.

Symbolically they are on the south side of Typical City, because most blacks in America were concentrated in the rural South before their movement to the cities in this century.

The heirs of continental European Protestantism, the descendants of people who did not speak English, are on the near northwest side. These are Lutheran, the Dutch Reformed, and the German Reformed which is now part of the United Church of Christ. Beyond them, also of continental background, are three in the family of dissenters: the Mennonites, Church of the Brethren, and Moravians.

The city was quite crowded by 1900, so later newcomers from eastern Europe had to crowd into old neighborhoods near downtown. These included the Jews, the only group in our story without Christian roots, and the Eastern Orthodox.

We can locate on the north end of town, not its richest section but a rapidly growing one, three churches "born in America": the Seventh-day Adventists, the Church of Christ, Scientist, and Jehovah's Witnesses. They have almost nothing in common with each other except that they were born in the United States and began to be well known just before the end of the 1800s.

At the same time other new movements sprang up and developed into new churches. These grew to be strong in the South and Southeast of our nation. We shall locate them in that part of Typical City, our miniature of the United States. These include the Salvation Army, the Pentecostal churches, and the family of fundamentalist churches.

Typical City had and has no room for the Native American church or other Christian or part-Christian American Indian religious bodies, so we shall represent them beyond the border of the city, as if on a reservation, to the west.

After the tour of the churches, we shall visit a few religious groups or themes that may not have houses of worship or may not be organized into denominations; they, too, are part of the story. But most of the story we can best imagine by picturing a building—a church, chapel, temple, cathedral, or storefront—and people coming in and going out—Americans, Christians, moderns, of many and marvelous sorts. ●

7 Church Architecture

Our church buildings do not all look alike. They reflect traditions from different times and places and different styles of worship. Modern churches sometimes use modern styles and newer building materials.

On our visits to the churches and synagogues of Typical City we will pay some attention to what the buildings look like. When you mention "church" to Americans, they do not usually picture just any old church. They picture *their* church. When they build new ones, they often say that they want "a church that looks like a church." No one can tell exactly what such a church should look like. What they usually mean is that they want a building which reminds them of one they grew up in, or one of the great ones they have visited.

America has produced a very large number of architectural styles, and all of them can be seen in almost any medium-sized city. Some

Barbara A. Benton

Quaker worship is plain, so Quaker meetinghouses, inside and outside, are plain.

23

Georgian architecture, above, developed in England 1714-1811, was common among colonial Episcopalians, most of whom had strong ties with England. Gothic churches, below, well-suited for the Catholic Mass, were especially popular among Catholics during the 1800s.

churches will look like New England meetinghouses. This means that they are white, wooden, quite bare, with clear windows. These are churches for the United Church of Christ, especially its former Congregationalists. Many community churches in the suburbs have copied this style. It does not work well for Catholics, though a few Catholics have adapted it. Catholics need somewhat more elaborate buildings for the Mass, and they like stained glass, some pictures, and statues.

A second style many Americans call Georgian. This came to America with the Episcopalians in Virginia and the Carolinas, and many of these grand churches still stand in Charleston, Williamsburg, and elsewhere. They are usually of red brick with white wood trim. The glass may be clear, but now the style is a bit more formal; kings have worshiped in such churches. There is a more elaborate table or altar for the Holy Communion.

A third style is the Gothic. The Gothic came to America chiefly in the middle of the nineteenth century during a time when architects talked about a "Gothic Revival." The Gothic was the elaborate form which grew up chiefly in northern Europe (among "the Goths," some thought). Its pointed arches were the main features. Gothic almost demands intricate stained glass to match its many decorative features. It is well styled for the Catholic Mass, since its relative darkness promotes formality and mystery. Many Protestants borrowed this style for churches in which preaching, not Mass, is the main act. This causes a problem, since it is hard to hear in most of these long, narrow, high churches.

For a time Americans favored "Greek Revival" architecture, with pillared facades of the sort used for banks, courthouses, and public buildings in the state and national capitals. These church buildings represented a sense of strength and endurance, even if their ancestors in Greece and Rome were not used for worship, certainly not for Christian worship.

In most American cities you can tell where various immigrant groups lived by studying the architecture. Immigrants brought along styles which reminded them of home. If they remembered a synagogue in Poland, they wanted one like it in the lower east side of New York. Catholics brought along styles which meant that a little bit of Italy, Spain, Ireland, or Germany would be represented on a city corner. These were often large, fortress-like buildings for which common people sacrificed much. The churches were havens, symbols of home, yet at the same time signs that the churches were in America to stay.

After World War II there was a great building boom. Then what people call contemporary or modern styles began to be built. In part this was a practical necessity. People could not afford the Gothic, and they could not even find stonecutters to help prepare the stone for Gothic buildings. The new buildings also took advantage of new materials and techniques, like reinforced concrete. Instead of lining people up in pews, many architects made it possible for worshipers to see each other in semicircles or round patterns. Artists were called in to prepare banners, statues, and windows. Most of all, however, they capture the idea that places of worship could, through simplicity and the proper arrangement of seating, light, and space, suggest the Holy. ●

Many places of worship built since World War II have used modern materials, such as concrete, and have been both creative and economical in design. Pictured here is St. John's Abbey Church, Collegeville, Minnesota.

Minneapolis Tribune

St. John's University

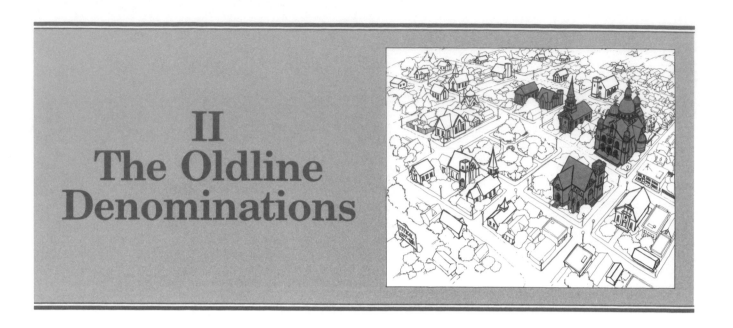

II
The Oldline Denominations

8 The Roman Catholics

James Cardinal Gibbons, 1834-1921
Friend of American Laborers

In the 1800s, many Catholics from different nations of Europe came to the United States. James Cardinal Gibbons, an important Catholic leader, supported the right of workers to organize labor unions and established an enduring bond between the Catholic Church and laborers.

This map shows regions in the United States where the majority of church members are Catholics.

Since there are 50 million American Catholics in 25,000 local parishes, a Catholic church is the most familiar place of worship in American landscapes or cityscapes. *Roman* Catholic—the name Protestants prefer to use because Protestants consider themselves to be "catholic" too—is the oldest Christian name in the Americas. Columbus brought over the Catholic Church with him. Soon after his arrival in 1492, priests and brothers were spreading Catholicism. Most of the Catholics were in Spanish America to the south or French America in the Canadian north, while the United States grew chiefly and at first out of 13 English-speaking Protestant colonies. Only about 20,000 Catholics lived in the colonies at the time of the Revolution, and almost all of these were in Maryland and southern Pennsylvania.

Catholicism spread throughout the country in the 1800s, thanks to immigration and strenuous work by priests, nuns, and lay leaders. Irish potato famines in the 1840s produced the first waves of Catholic immigrants. Later, Catholics came from Germany and from Italy, Poland, and other nations of southern and eastern Europe. Yet many of them were quite passive church members in Europe and had to be activated in America. The first American bishop, John Carroll, had to work chiefly with imported priests. Soon he and his successors helped found seminaries and attracted young immigrant men to them. A supply of priests grew. Many religious orders of men and women started schools and hospitals. The Catholic Church was ready for the great turn of the century immigrations.

The missionary priests met the boats and involved the people. Soon city and country skylines alike were graced with grand churches and high steeples. The immigrants, though often poor, sacrificed for these churches. Under their roofs they found a warm welcome, people who cared, persons who spoke their language, others with whom to be sociable. Catholics soon learned from Protestants how to have a network of charities and relief agencies. Churches became social centers for clubs, dances, meeting marriage partners, and celebrating the joys and facing the sorrows of life.

Catholic people needed each other because other Americans were often hostile. In the 1800s, during the years of the great immigrations, Pope Pius IX and other European Catholic leaders reacted against liberalism and revolution in France and other European nations. They said very harsh things about democracy. Enemies of Catholicism who remembered religious wars in Europe really did fear the pope, or they made use of other people's fears to stir up anti-Catholic hatred. In the 1830s and 1840s, a mob in Charlestown near Boston burned a convent school, and in Philadelphia anti-Irish-Catholic riots took some lives. In contrast to Europe's religious wars, these were minor incidents. However, in contrast to America's promises of religious freedom and concord, they were serious shortcomings.

Catholicism needed strong leadership. Some lay people provided it. Among these was the first American-born saint, Mother Ann Seton (1774-1821). Clergy, especially bishops, were best positioned to lead, however. The greatest such person in United States history was James Cardinal Gibbons (1834-1921). He was archbishop of Baltimore from 1877 to 1921, the crucial years for Catholic immigration.

Gibbons was a diplomat who tried to rule not with an iron hand but with what he called "masterly inactivity." He encouraged members to let things happen, and he himself let things happen, forbidding only outrageous violations.

Gibbons wanted the immigrant Catholics to be truly American. He was known as a patriot, a nationalist, and a friend of presidents. He wanted America to be a host to Catholics, and he worked tirelessly to show the nation how well Catholicism fit in. The greatest favor he did Catholicism and the Church in general was to be a quiet friend of the labor movement. In the years of his leadership the cities and factories were growing. "Robber barons," wealthy men with weak consciences, held power over the workers and exploited them in their poverty. The workers wanted to organize. One of their instruments was a fraternity, the Knights of Labor. Stubborn old-time Catholics thought that movements such as secret societies would be enemies of the Church. Gibbons fought all the way to Rome for permission for Catholics to belong. He prevailed, and the laborers of America remained friendly to the Church, while in Europe most were lost to the faith. ●

Catholics settled primarily in cities. Newcomers often established new neighborhoods or moved into neighborhoods already populated by people of their nationality.

9 Catholics since the Second Vatican Council

The Second Vatican Council has profoundly affected Catholic life and worship, teaching methods, church architecture, the roles of priests and lay people, and attitudes toward other Christians.

In order to understand religion in America, a person almost has to make two stops for Catholics: one at an old church where the grandparents were brought up and one at a new church where their grandchildren are.

The great change came when Pope John XXIII called an ecumenical council that met in Rome between 1962 and 1965. This gathering of the world's Catholic bishops is usually named the Second Vatican Council or Vatican II. Pope John and his successor Pope Paul VI wanted to preserve the Church's basic doctrines but also to update the Church so that it could speak more clearly in the modern world. Pope John called this movement *aggiornamento,* an "updating," a rearrangement of furniture, an opening of windows.

Through the decrees (laws) of Vatican II, the Church got rid of some outdated practices from earlier centuries. Even the appearance of Catholic churches has changed. Once upon a time Catholic altars were placed up against the wall. The priest prayed with his back to the people, symbolically turned to God, to Christ as present in the Host or sacred bread. Since Vatican II, however, the altar table has been moved forward, away from the wall, and the priest faces the people.

Whereas the priest used to say Mass in the Latin language, today he celebrates Mass in English, or in the common language of the people. Once upon a time, only ordained people took part in the liturgy of the Mass. Today, in most dioceses, lay men and women read Scripture, lead singing, and distribute Communion at Mass. Before the Council, nuns always wore long, usually dark dresses and veils that covered their hair completely. Priests always wore black clerical suits or long black robes called cassocks. Today, most nuns and priests dress in contemporary styles.

And there are more differences. Grandfather Catholic will tell you how he was never allowed to eat meat on Friday; granddaughter may eat it. Grandmother will remember that she was never allowed to attend a Protestant church service and never expected to see Protestants in her church. Last year when her grandson married a Presbyterian, the Presbyterian minister joined her priest to help in the marriage rite. Such joint activity is a result of the Council's Decree on Ecumenism, which calls on Catholics to encourage the ecumenical movement toward Christian unity.

Not all the changes after the Second Vatican Council are visible to the eye of someone visiting a church. But whoever watches the whole Church in America does notice many changes. The seminaries and universities have a variety of approaches to Catholic teaching or doctrine. It may be that some Protestants teach in the religion departments of Catholic colleges. Some Catholics feel freer to disagree with their leaders than before.

The Catholic Church has undergone profound changes. Still, Catholics cherish many of the same traditions as did their ancestors. They look to the *magisterium,* or official teaching authority of the Church, for guidance in living. They revere leaders like Pope John Paul II as much as they honored his predecessors—and they may even have seen him, since recent popes leave their home in the Vatican to travel.

Since the Second Vatican Council, Catholicism has been in turmoil as liberals and conservatives have opposed one another. Yet a new spirit of openness has entered the Church. The Church grows, the faithful remain, and the Church, now more varied than ever, looks for new ways to serve the cities and the world. ●

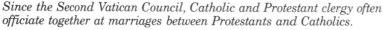

Since the Second Vatican Council, Catholic and Protestant clergy often officiate together at marriages between Protestants and Catholics.

10 The United Church of Christ: The Congregational Heritage

Congregationalism—the religion of the Puritans and Pilgrims—was a major religious influence in the early years of America. This group today often leads Christian involvement in social issues. In 1957, the Congregational churches became part of a new church body, the United Church of Christ.

In 1957 the Congregational Church, one of the big three colonial churches, joined with the Evangelical and Reformed Church to form the United Church of Christ. So today you will seldom see the word "Congregational" in an American city. In the 1980s, there are about 1.7 million United Church of Christ members in 6,000 local churches, and the median age of members is over 55. Perhaps 600 local churches that keep the name "Congregational" chose not to merge into the United Church of Christ. They feared that their belief in the authority of the local congregation would be bargained away in the merger; otherwise they do not differ much from their kin churches who did let the name disappear.

Although Congregationalism is relatively small today, it had a strong head start in America and played a major part in religious history in the United States. Children who learn about the Puritans and Pilgrims are remembering the Congregationalists. The American who sends a Christmas card or looks at a calendar with a white New England village meetinghouse on it is honoring an almost mythical national church style. The picture will be of a Congre-

The founding of Yale, above, and Harvard, below, shows Congregational concern for higher education.

gational church. The simplicity of the interior of the meetinghouse seems especially "American."

In the 1780s the president of Yale—like Harvard College, a product of the Congregationalists—predicted that one-third of America, the North, would be Congregational. Yet two hundred years later, only about 13 out of 1,000 American church members belong to the United Church of Christ, a body which includes more than Congregationalists. However, the tradition has importance beyond its numbers.

Congregationalism was started by English Protestants who resented bishops and any control from above the local body of Christians—except from God. They believed they were in a covenant with God, and that each local congregation could best interpret this covenant and live by it. They gave great power to laity and local preachers, though they might "consociate" or band together for some causes. Congregationalists first came to New England in 1620 (as Separatist Pilgrims) and 1630 (as more churchly Puritans) and peopled the villages, establishing their churches by law. When America was born in 1776, there were 749 Congregational churches, far more than the Presbyterians, the second largest church group with 495.

Congregationalism values preaching and learning in its ministry. But as America moved west, this group of churches did not mobilize well to compete for the heart of frontier people. They lost faith in revivalism and worked chiefly with the educated few, through whom their religion influenced cities. They built great colleges. Yet they did not capture the imagination of those who wanted their preachers to promote conversions.

The Congregationalist vision was well shared by Horace Bushnell (1802-1876). This notable thinker opposed revivalism. As we see in his book *Christian Nurture,* Bushnell wanted children to be seen as Christians in miniature, who needed to be tutored and nurtured for growth in faith. This Yale-educated preacher charmed highly informed people who thought revivalists were ill-mannered and rude. With Bushnell as a leader, Congregationalists were less concerned about the boundaries between those who were "saved" and those who were "unsaved." This message appealed to the college

Educator Horace Bushnell (1802-1876) believed that children grow in Christian faith through nurture and education rather than through sudden conversion and revivals.

trained and the well-off and well-mannered. The common people welcomed Bushnell's enthusiastic preaching about how God was working in the Civil War through the armies of the North. They did not think he was very realistic, however, when he implied that people could be quite good without having a conversion experience.

Congregationalism, first under that name, and then in the United Church of Christ, quietly continues to make its way. It stresses education for ministry. The men and women in its ministry tend to be very much at home in American culture. They are likely to be ready for experiment in the arts. When a new idea comes along and most Christians are tentative and cautious, Congregationalists want to give it a hearing.

The vitalities of Congregationalism show up chiefly in debate over the great issues of the day. This is a denomination where homosexual rights, the care of the earth against its spoilers, the causes of justice and peace, will get a hearing. Christians who want churches that have, figuratively, high walls and thick boundaries are likely to go elsewhere. Christians who stay will find themselves in the service of a God who, they believe, does not want to be cooped up in creeds or customs—and does not want the people to be, either.

11 The Unitarian Universalists

The Unitarian Church in the United States was started in the early 1800s by Congregationalists who questioned some of their church's beliefs about God and Jesus. William Ellery Channing was an important early leader among Unitarians. The Unitarian and Universalist Churches merged in 1961.

William Ellery Channing, 1780-1842
Early Leader Among Unitarians

One of the old downtown churches with roots in colonial America is the Unitarian Universalist congregation. Most Americans know the name "Unitarian," but not many have direct contact with its worship and ways. The denomination is very small. There are 350 Catholics for every Unitarian in America, and Unitarian Universalist Association churches are present in fewer than 1,000 communities. Their denomination grew up on Christian soil, in America chiefly out of New England Congregationalism. Yet members today believe that truth and light can come from many sources—Buddha or Akhnaton or Jean-Paul Sartre as well as Moses or Jesus—so they do not want to be confined in the Judeo-Christian traditions. So broad is this church that it is also a home for humanists, people who believe there are no higher sources of value than humans themselves. Humanists see no need to use the name God.

For all their distance from traditional Christianity, the Unitarians, where they are present, like to make themselves heard. In some respects, they are closer to the faith of some American founders like Thomas Jefferson, Benjamin Franklin, and George Washington, than are most other churches. Like these founders, they have a respect for Jesus without seeing him as the divine Son of God. Along with the eighteenth-century statesmen, they also have respect for the moral patterns taught in much of the Bible. Yet they do not believe in miracles or see the book as supernatural. With the founders, they ordinarily have great faith in human reason. Just as the leaders of two centuries ago celebrated progress and nature, their heirs today like to bring inquiry and science into their churches.

The visitor to a Unitarian Universalist assembly may be thrown off because some aspects of the gathering are similar to what goes on in a more conventional church; yet so much is different. There are not likely to be any crosses or pictures drawn from biblical scenes. There will be a sermon, more likely on an urgent topic of the day than on a biblical text. Music will have its place, but a Hindemith flute sonata is as likely as a great chorale or hymn. Ordinarily there will be no sacraments, though some churches have rituals of initiation and fellowship that fill the space in life that baptism and the Lord's Supper fill for Christians.

Many New England Congregational churches in the early 1800s turned Unitarian under Harvard-trained ministers. They took their church buildings with them.

The man who, more than any other, gave voice to conservative Unitarianism was William Ellery Channing (1780-1842), one of the most gifted speakers and writers of America. He would not recognize today's humanistic Unitarians. Channing might not know what to make of a religious gathering that slights the Bible but that might read Hindu texts or hear an agnostic scientist from the pulpit. Yet he would join the members in celebrating free inquiry and love of truth.

Channing was a calm, almost timid man, but he was bold in his rejection of Calvinism. He thought that version of faith depicted an angry and capricious God who sent unbaptized babies to eternal torment and who bred pride in those who called themselves elect, chosen. Channing thought Jesus was special, the highest human, but not a unique Son of God. As he preached these themes, he was more and more excluded from Congregationalism. In 1815, as the Unitarian denomination formed, many looked to him for leadership.

Channing's God was reasonable, though still supernatural, unlike the God of many later Unitarians. God was also good, as John Calvin's God did not seem to be. Humans were not blighted by original sin. Instead they had great potential for good, if only they would use reason to back their morals. Channing, a Harvard graduate who preached at Federal Street Congregational Church in Boston from 1803-1842, involved himself with anti-slavery and other social causes of the day.

Universalism in the 19th century looked like a rural version of the Unitarianism found in the cities. The Universalists believed that there was salvation, but that no one would be excluded from it. On these terms Universalist revivalists did battle with the Baptists and Methodists and their messages about a God who to Universalists sounded whimsical and petty.

In 1961 the Unitarian and Universalist traditions merged after years of negotiation over forms of governance. In these two church bodies that thus became one, if reason is in control, most members are quite happy. ●

*King's Chapel, Boston, which in 1785 became
the first Unitarian church in America*

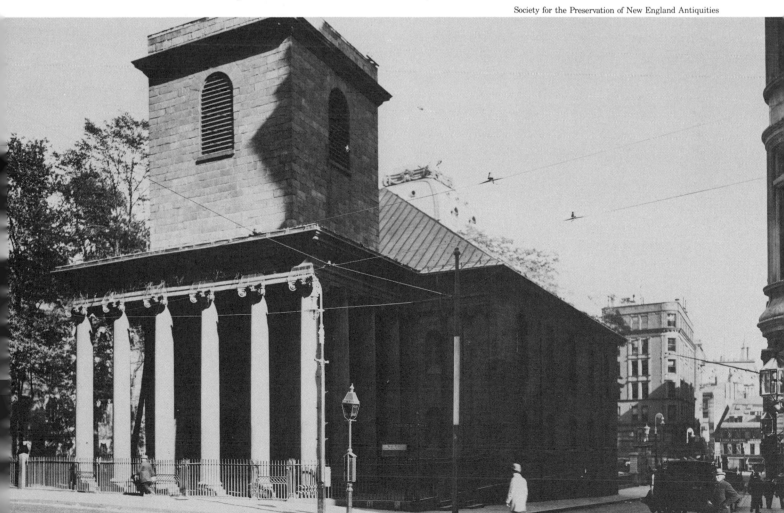

Charles Hodge, professor at Princeton Seminary, insisted that Presbyterian doctrines should not be changed. A portrait of John Calvin hangs on the wall in this drawing of Hodge and his students.

12 The Presbyterians

Presbyterians, a major group in the 1700s, have always valued educated clergy. Charles Hodge, a famous teacher of the 1800s, was known for his insistence on strict Presbyterian doctrine. Today the Presbyterian Church is more moderate but still centers its worship and teaching on the Bible.

Only about three out of 100 American church members are Presbyterian, but Presbyterians are influential beyond their numbers. While this church serves the common people, it also has provided much leadership in the business world, in corporate America. You will find a Presbyterian church downtown in Typical City, for people of this version of Christian faith have been around for a long time. Their churches may be rather grand, often in Gothic styles. The pulpit will be prominent.

Presbyterians have a long tradition of splitting up, a habit reaching back to Scotland, the homeland of many of their ancestors. In 1861 American Presbyterians separated over slavery and secession. It was not until 1983 that the northern and southern branches came back together. The one new body is called the Presbyterian Church in the United States of America.

Presbyterianism was one of the "big three" colonial Protestant churches. To the north were Congregationalists and to the south Episcopalians, in churches supported by state law. In Scotland, Presbyterianism was the official faith.

But Presbyterians came to the middle colonies too late to be the church established by law. Many of the arrivals in the decades before the American Revolution were Scotch-Irish, people of Scottish descent sent by England to settle in Ireland in the 1600s as a force against Catholicism. They were a rough and hardy breed, ready for the American frontier. Many of them, finding coastal cities full, carried Presbyterianism westward.

From early in the 1700s Presbyterians were attracted to two competing styles of church life. Some of them were staunchly orthodox. They held to John Calvin's stern message that told them they were God's elect and that God held them accountable for their own morals and his truth. Between 1741 and 1758 there rose some rough-and-ready revivalists who split with the traditional party. These Presbyterians worked the frontier with an emotional message of conversion. They did battle for souls against the devil, false teaching, and the Methodists alike. The combination worked, and Presbyterianism grew, but not as fast as the Methodist and Baptist churches.

Presbyterians have kept their image as upholders of Christian doctrine. They cherished a "learned ministry," even in the frontier days when Methodist and Baptist preachers were often nearly illiterate but more ready to ride the circuit. A Presbyterian stronghold was Princeton Seminary in New Jersey. Charles Hodge (1797-1878), as well as anyone, shows what learned Presbyterians thought their church should be.

Born in Philadelphia, Charles Hodge studied at Princeton and then in Europe: at Paris, Halle, and Berlin. From 1820 to 1878 he towered over the Princeton faculty and glowered at any who wanted to dot a Presbyterian doctrinal *i* differently or who failed to cross one of the *t*'s. He boasted, against modern-minded thinkers, that no new idea entered Princeton while he was there. In his view, the old ideas were best. He studied the old imported Presbyterian doctrines and taught them to students. To him, the Christian faith was a matter of common sense. His books, journals, and articles, as well as some 3,000 graduates, carried his firm outlook to the churches of the country. His seminary later provided some of the ideas that today make up fundamentalism, a rigid reaction to modern religious ideas.

The spirit of Hodge never disappeared, yet most Presbyterian churches are not known for this conservatism. People go to them to hear preaching, an art which Presbyterian seminaries work hard to develop in graduates. The biblical departments of such schools are strong, for the preachers are expected to develop themes from biblical texts. Though John Calvin was a bit uneasy with the arts, modern Presbyterianism has often cultivated the arts in a way that early Calvinists could not have foreseen.

Presbyterians have been, by and large, an educated church, despite the frontier origins of so many members. Their literacy has helped give them positions of prominence. Several presidents, among them Woodrow Wilson and Dwight Eisenhower, have been Presbyterians. As mainline Protestants, even conservative Presbyterians are open to politics and the debate over ideas in the culture. They argue with each other over world affairs, the rights of homosexuals and ministry to them, and the ways to face world hunger or to deal with nuclear arms. At heart, however, Presbyterians want to be known for biblical faithfulness and for feeling at home in a United States that their ancestors helped found. ●

Presbyterians founded Princeton University, shown below in an old engraving. Woodrow Wilson (1856-1924), a president of Princeton, became President of the United States in 1913.

13 The Episcopalians

After the Revolution, the Episcopal Church—because it had such strong ties to England—had to start over again. John Henry Hobart was a leader during these years. The Episcopal Church is rich in traditions of music and worship, and gives much prominence to Holy Communion.

Downtown in many an American city, the Episcopal church stands as a landmark to the days when people of English parentage dominated American religion. Anglicanism, which became Episcopalianism in America, was the official religion of the English nation when the American colonies were first settled. Those who came to Virginia and the Carolinas brought this church with them as naturally as they brought the English language and ways of life. They established it by law.

In recent times, only a few more than 20 out of a 1,000 American church members belong to the Episcopal Church. Yet this church is better known and possesses more influence than its numbers might suggest. A church rich in pageantry and form—Americans who are not Episcopal know it best from television images that deal with the British monarchy at worship—it favors styles of worship that appeal to educated people, often those of wealth, and those who care for the arts. The sermon means less to most Episcopalians than to, say, Presbyterian or Baptist church members. But Holy Communion has more prominence. Roman Catholics often feel at home in Episcopal worship, which sometimes is "higher" and more formal than Catholic liturgy since the Second Vatican Council.

Bishop John Henry Hobart, 1775-1830
"High Church" Episcopal Leader

Episcopalianism, which today holds the loyalty of 2.8 million people in over 7,000 parishes, has been known as the church of the rich and the famous. More presidents have come from this communion than any other, and most of the Founding Fathers—George Washington, Patrick Henry, George Mason, James Madison, and the like—were members. During their time, their church had room for a kind of rationalism, in contrast to the emotionalism of many churches. Episcopalians believed that God was reasonable and benevolent. This was a religion of manners and polish.

After the Revolution the Episcopal Church almost had to start from scratch. Many of the clergy were Tory, Loyalists to the British crown against the American Revolutionaries. The southern parishes were poor, and even though they were established, the churches had often failed to support their priests well. After the war Samuel Seabury, consecrated in Scotland, became the first American bishop. He and soon some colleagues gave leadership, profiting from a revival of formalism in the Anglican communion in England. ("Communion" is sometimes used to mean church body or denomination.)

We glimpse the new model best in John Henry Hobart (1775-1830), Philadelphia-born bishop of New York from 1811 to 1830 and teacher in General Theological Seminary, New York. The Episcopal Church was divided between those who wanted it to look as plain and Protestant as possible and those who had more "Catholic" interests. Hobart gave forceful leadership to the high church, or Catholic, side. He preached well, stirring educated people who were left cold by the emotionalism of revivalists. Hobart recalled the glories of the English church tradition, of Catholic doctrine, of formal liturgy. Sometimes he was authoritarian and made unnecessary enemies, but his way tended to prevail.

While Hobart and his kind awakened enemies in "low church" Episcopalianism, they also bred mistrust among other Protestants. To them the new Episcopal style looked like an imitation of "popish" Roman Catholic ways. Many Americans believed that the true church would be the one that was simplest and most primitive. Though Episcopalians called themselves Protestants, in the eyes of some Americans they had departed from the plainness of New Testament Christianity. The revivalists in other churches often disapproved, because they saw no reason for elaborate vestments; Gothic architecture; or the ranks of bishop, priest, and deacon. What made the revived Episcopalianism more acceptable was that, through preachers like Hobart, the warmth of the Christian gospel shone through.

The Episcopal Church has kept its various high and low church parties. From its beginning in England in 1534, this church believed in "comprehension," its ability to include people of differing kinds of commitments. It would be misleading to see this denomination as only wealthy and aristocratic. Its missionaries worked hard among the American Indians, and many went willingly to foreign lands. There are Episcopal churches on reservations, in barren little towns, and in the slums.

The Episcopal Church, rich in traditions of music and worship, is very much in the Protestant mainline. This means that its members are at home in the general culture, not eager to live inside fortresses of faith. Lacking an interest in evangelism, their church does not prosper as the more fervent ones do. Yet it continues to contribute much through its style of life and outlook and its connection to the worldwide Anglican communion.

George Washington

James Monroe

Franklin Delano Roosevelt

The four presidents pictured here were Episcopalians.

The National Episcopal Cathedral in Washington, D.C., is a symbol of religion's place in America's national life. Although an Episcopal place of worship, it is often used for events that have national as we well as denominational meaning.

Gerald Ford

III
The Oldline Dissenting Denominations

14 The Baptists of the North

Brown Brothers

Roger Williams, 1603?-1684
Early Baptist Leader, Founder of Rhode Island,
and Advocate of Religious Freedom

Baptists in America never depended upon the government for support. Baptists grew rapidly during the late 1700s and became the largest Protestant church family in America. The Social Gospel and faithfulness to the Bible are among strong Baptist traditions.

There are many Baptist church bodies in America, in many sizes and shapes. An encyclopedia lists over fifty groups, some with colorful names like "Two-Seed-in-the-Spirit Predestinarian Baptists" or the "Duck River (and Kindred) Association of Baptists." Nineteen out of 100 American church members are Baptist. One in three of these is black. Among white Baptists, the vast majority are either in the 1.5-

million-member American Baptist Churches in the U.S.A. or the huge Southern Baptist Convention. (Several Baptist groups call themselves conventions, because they want to be thought of as collections of local churches more than as denominations.)

The group now officially called the American Baptist Churches in the U.S.A. claims ancestry all the way back to Roger Williams and First Baptist Church in Providence, Rhode Island, 1638. Yet Baptist churches, old as they are, began their life in America on different terms than did Episcopalians, Congregationalists, and Presbyterians. They were outsiders in colonial times, protesters and dissenters against the official churches. They naturally went first to Rhode Island, which allowed religious freedom—to which they contributed. Later they won a place in the rest of New England by refusing to pay taxes or to support established churches, sometimes going to jail, preaching fervently, and starting hundreds of small churches. Then they fanned into the South and West.

Already by the time of the birth of the nation in 1776 there were 457 of these Baptist churches. This meant that they ranked third among the denominations in number of congregations. They were ready to compete with Methodists on the frontier.

It is hard to tell the visitor what to expect in Baptist congregations of the North. Because these churches are congregational, they decide most things for themselves. Some may be almost fundamentalist or doctrinal traditionalists, and others may be quite liberal or experimental. Not all northern Baptists hold to old Baptist demands. For example, Baptists have traditionally reserved baptism for believing adults, and have baptized by immersion. But one may now even become a member without being immersed as an adult.

The Baptists, reflecting their battles against the churchly establishment and for "soul freedom," make freedom their great theme. They want to be faithful to biblical teaching, but they also want freedom of religion, freedom of choice, freedom to change the world. That last theme has put many northern Baptists into the camps of progressive Christians. When we look for someone who embodies the Baptist vision, the best choice may be the Social Gospel minister, Professor Walter Rauschenbusch.

Baptists practice baptism by immersion of persons considered old enough to believe for themselves.

While most Baptists were of English roots, there are also Scandinavian and German Baptists. Walter Rauschenbusch (1861-1918), born at Rochester, New York, was from the family of a German Baptist minister. He spent eleven years before 1897 as a minister in "Hell's Kitchen," an immigrant area of poverty and high crime in New York City. There he came to love the common people and to see human needs that fashionable Christianity usually overlooked. Rauschenbusch did not want to depend on charity alone to deal with these needs, however. He felt the economic system was wrong. It did not allow for cooperation. Too few capitalists controlled too much wealth and too many lives. While Rauschenbusch did not favor violent revolution or class warfare, he did support socialism in much of American life and industry.

Walter Rauschenbusch (1861-1918), leader of the Social Gospel movement, tried to relate Christianity to an industrial society.

Rauschenbusch taught church history at Rochester Seminary. There he read texts from the biblical prophets, admired John the Baptist, and wanted to follow Jesus. He thought medieval dissenters and earlier Baptists, because they loved freedom and because they were outsiders, were models for changing the system. His dream was to "bring in the Kingdom of God." Rauschenbusch and his friends in the Social Gospel movement were not successful. They were, it was said, too socialist for most Christians, and too Christian for most socialists. Unlike many Catholic leaders they were not close to many laborers. Yet their dream of a Kingdom and their preaching of righteousness had an influence on legislation. Years later Martin Luther King, Jr., was to be inspired by Rauschenbusch and others in his Baptist tradition.

Today, Baptists of the American Baptist Churches network are among the old downtown churches of the mainline. While many moved to the suburbs, they were not in the forefront of the planting of new churches. The revivals that helped them get started are now rare events. They put their energies into worship that stresses preaching more than baptism or Communion. The health of the Baptist tradition differs very much from congregation to congregation, from locality to locality. And while lay members may be no more politically liberal than other Christians, they do give liberal preachers a hearing as these men and women preach social justice. What else can Baptists do? They stand for freedom to preach, to hear, to agree, to disagree, and then—having made up their minds—to act in Christ's name.

15 The Society of Friends, or Quakers

In the Society of Friends, or Quakers, simplicity is the main mark of worship. Members wait in silence for the inspiration of the Spirit. Though their membership is small, Quakers are well known for their activities on behalf of peace and social justice.

If it lives up to its image, the most modest and simple church in town will be the Friends Meeting House. While modern members of the Society of Friends can express themselves with many styles, their tradition calls them to have the most plain kind of building. A visitor to other Christian churches in town will have built up a certain number of expectations based on seeing many similarities from church to church. The Friends building will be surprising, in that case.

There will not be an altar, since these Christians do not say Mass or celebrate Holy Communion. They will have no font or pool for baptizing, because they also do not believe that baptism is valid. Bread, wine, and water are "external" things, and the rites that come with them are "external ordinances." Friends want to stress the inward light and way, the Spirit, and nothing external.

When Quakers come together on "First Day," they usually sit in silence until someone is moved by the Spirit to rise and speak.

The visitor who looks for stained glass, paintings, organs, and pulpits will be disappointed. In most cases the eavesdropper on Quaker worship will not find a pastor, either. But it is misleading to continue this list of "what is missing" in Friends circles. Those who belong have a much different view: They stress what is there, what they have, which they feel other Christians lose when they became so formal and showy.

Not long after they began in the back country of England in the 1650s, these Friends gained another name. Friends were often put on trial by their enemies. In court they took no oaths, but warned people to "tremble" in the presence of God. People outside the Friends came to call them "Quakers," a name still used today.

They came soon to America, where they were often persecuted. Pacifists in the Revolutionary War, they did not seem to be likely prospects for survival. Yet here they are in Typical City, one local group out of the 125,000 Quaker people in America.

When Quakers come together at their meeting house on "First Day," at an appointed time, they usually sit in silence until someone arises to give witness or testimony, as the Spirit moves. They believe in "that of God in every one." If no one feels prompted to speak on a particular day, they all part with a handshake and go their ways. If someone is prompted to speak, they listen respectfully and then part with a handshake. There may be readings in such a service, but do not expect a bulletin announcing an Order of Worship!

Quakers are well known for settling their differences through "consensus" or agreement, something very difficult to reach. They do not believe in power-play votes, but seek the solutions through arguments based upon gentle persuasion. Sometimes the approach works, sometimes it does not.

Modern Friends are best known by the public at large for their peace witness. Today not all Friends are pacifists, but it is rare for them to be strongly pro-war or pro-defense. The American Friends Service Committee, an expression of some Friends and their friends (for not all AFSC members are Quakers), is also well regarded for works of care and welfare.

Friends come in several denominational forms, from the more or less Pentecostal to moderate and liberal. Few Friends believe there should be a denominational creed. They cherish the Bible not because they prove it to be true but because they find truth in it.

Peter Stettenheim; courtesy of Friends Journal

A typical Friends' meetinghouse is shown below. Usually, this church is the simplest and plainest one in town.

16 American Churches as Changers of Their World

Christian churches try to change the world. Churches encourage people to improve personal morals. Churches also try to correct social wrongs, such as slavery, poverty, and bad working conditions.

Critics remind the churches that they are supposed to exist not only for their own members but for the world around them as well. Surely some churches live mainly for themselves. But the American churches also have people of vision, who believe that they should change the world. Even though Americans separated church and state, this separation did not mean that churches could take no part in public life.

The churches have gone through many phases and stages in their efforts to change the world. The first one, and still the most powerful, is to concentrate on individual morals. So the churches have asked individuals to stop being profane, stop drinking, and stop reading obscene literature. All this is part of what Methodist founder John Wesley called "spreading scriptural holiness throughout the land." No one can ever measure how different America would be if church members individually did not try to live better lives. Or how much different it would be if more of them succeeded!

Another way Christians have tried to change the world is to help the poor and needy. When there is a depression or times are hard, a good Catholic church opens its kitchens and asks members to donate food. A downtown Presbyterian church is likely to have a soup line. Less visible are the efforts churches make to find jobs for the unemployed or to help out their own or their neighbors' families in need.

But large-scale problems often demand larger solutions than a parish can provide, so Americans have developed many organizations or as-

Christians try both to help the needy and to attack causes of poverty and injustice.

Theodore Weld (1803-1895), below, challenged Christians to fight more fiercely against the evil of slavery.

sociations. Thus the Young Men's Christian Association, born in London in 1844 and imported seven years later to America, started as a base in the city for young Christians. Here were offered Bible study, inexpensive living, recreation, a home away from home. The Y.M.C.A. trained missionaries to go overseas. Gradually the word "Christian" came to mean less in the cement over the door. Most people do not think of the Y.M.C.A. as an agency of churches, but once it was.

The Volunteers of America, which split off from the Salvation Army in 1896, provides medical aid and food to those who cannot afford these. "Meals on Wheels" is a way church people in hundreds of communities have of taking out meals to sick and aged or lonely people who have no money, no friends, no transportation, or no health. Christians have also organized in recent years to help those far away. For example, to combat hunger around the world we have groups like the mainline Church World Service, the evangelical World Vision, and Catholic Relief Services.

Some Christians want to do more than change individual morals or help the needy. They want to take on the difficult task of changing the patterns of society that they consider wrong. In the 1800s many in the churches of the North became abolitionists, working to do away with slavery. Theodore Dwight Weld was a typical radical agitator. When the famous minister Lyman Beecher came to the semi-southern city of Cincinnati in the 1830s to lead Lane Seminary, a Presbyterian school, he had to contend with Weld, a student there. Beecher was against slavery and worked moderately against it, but Weld was more impatient. Weld confronted Beecher, much as dissident students in America faced their university officials during the 1960s and 1970s to protest the Vietnam War. Beecher was worried about the good will of Cincinnatians and wanted to go slow. Weld left Lane and took almost the whole student body with him to Oberlin College. There the fiery abolitionist helped train students to go on the revival trail, preaching the need for abolition.

In the second half of the nineteenth century and early in the twentieth century, many Christians were concerned about alcoholic beverages. Drinking of alcohol was not only a personal problem but also a social one. Saloon-keepers placed their businesses at mine and

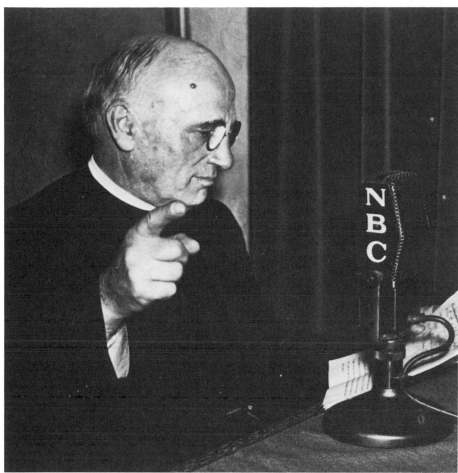

Monsignor John Ryan, giving a nationwide radio talk in 1936, defended the policies of President Franklin D. Roosevelt. Ryan strongly supported industrial workers and spoke against child labor.

factory entrances, and soon many men were losing their paychecks and becoming addicted. Their families became destitute. To stop this, churches worked to prohibit the manufacture and sale of alcoholic beverages.

In the late 1800s, many Protestant thinkers decided that while America had many Christian churches and good families and schools, the economic order was not Christianized. Competition, they charged, was vicious and worked against brotherhood. Laborers were not free to organize unions. So they developed the Social Gospel, which cut across denominational lines and united their activities. One early twentieth-century Social Gospel leader was Washington Gladden, a Congregationalist minister in Columbus, Ohio. He persuaded his members to side with labor in their struggle with management. The Social Gospel people and their powerful counterparts in Roman Catholic social movements worked on American consciences and helped produce change.

In the 1930s Protestant and Catholic leaders, led by people like Reinhold Niebuhr and Monsignor John Ryan, supported workers who wanted to organize and united to support government programs like those of President Franklin D. Roosevelt's New Deal.

In the 1960s Martin Luther King, Jr., a black Baptist, was the great leader working to bring about a change for racial justice. He preached the values of the Declaration of Independence, which taught equality. King learned nonviolence from Mohandas Gandhi in India, who imitated the Hebrew prophets and announced Jesus' call for righteousness. Thanks to such efforts, the nation passed new civil rights legislation. Churches also produced dissenters against the War in Vietnam, supporters of wars on poverty and hunger, and champions of better housing.

In the 1970s and 1980s some Christians took up the causes of nuclear disarmament, a better environment, and improved health care. These causes required more effort than any single congregation could muster, but many church bodies produced members, leaders, and agencies which, united, helped change America. ●

17 Getting New Members: The Revivalist Style

*Charles G. Finney, 1792-1875
The First Great American Revivalist*

The work of revivalist preachers has resulted in great growth for Protestant churches. Colorful evangelists have included Charles Finney, Dwight Moody, Billy Sunday, and Billy Graham.

All churches, including the Catholic, had to recruit immigrants and frontier people aggressively. But most Protestant church growth in America occurred as the result of efforts by evangelists or revivalists.

The revival style was set in colonial times under men like England's George Whitefield (1714-1770), who visited all the colonies, and Congregationalist Jonathan Edwards (1703-1758), who stayed with a Massachusetts parish and preached conversion there. With the opening of the frontier, new approaches developed.

One of the first giants of revivalism was Charles Grandison Finney (1792-1875), a New York lawyer who was converted to Presbyterianism but paid little attention to its doctrines. He was later told that as a Presbyterian he had accepted creeds that said God condemned unbaptized babies to hell. He could not believe that his denomination's statements said this, but he read the creeds and found out that they did. "I was shocked." Yet he remained Presbyterian.

Finney was successful with revivals in the smaller cities of New York state, but he knew he must also eventually take on the unchurched in New York, Boston, and the other great cities. For this, church buildings would not do. He used theaters and filled them with people who came to him as if for entertainment.

Entertain Finney did. With the support of rich merchants like the Philadelphia family of Wanamakers, who had their employees serve as ushers, he put on a great performance. As he saw it, each conversion cost only a few dollars and a certain amount of energy.

The colorful evangelist had great success. He turned over his converts to the churches. In his view, people were not passive. Indeed they had almost unlimited ability to carry out the works of God. As years passed, he also asked himself how revivalist energies could be put to work in the world. He became a moderate supporter of abolition.

A second in the gallery of great recruiters for the church was layman Dwight L. Moody (1837-1899), who came west to become a Chicago salesman. Converted, he was soon bringing children from slums to Sunday school, then teaching and preaching himself. Moody perfected city-style revivalism. He used great halls to gather huge crowds, made up mostly of the already converted. Moody commuted between America and England, building up crowds and getting converts. His style had entertainment value; people enjoyed coming to hear his blend of threats and promises. Early in his life he preached more about hellfire. Later he talked more about heaven. He did not care as much as Finney about changing the world. He preached a message of the imminent end of the world with Jesus' second coming. Comparing himself to Noah, Moody said he was bringing a lifeboat to rescue many in a world flooded by sin.

Third was Billy Sunday (1862-1935), the most crude and sensational of all the great revivalists. He had been a professional baseball player, and after his conversion he stopped at nothing to get crowds. The press found him a favorite and never tired of reporting on his wild language and the way he denounced liberals and modern morals. It is questionable whether Sunday built up the churches; he instead attracted crowds for himself.

A fourth in the tradition, which has also included many lesser figures, is Billy Graham. He came to prominence after World War II, when many thought the era of revivalism was over outside the South. Graham came from the South, but he had successes in cities like Los Angeles and New York. Graham started out regularly announcing the end of the world within a year or so. Through the years, however, people began to note a change in him. He helped make fundamentalism more open-minded. Some mainline Protestants became friendly. Many Catholics came to support him. Graham racially integrated his southern rallies before such mixing was a common event. Graham golfed with and became a pastor to presidents. Yet Graham's main service was to keep the gospel message of the churches alive in the secular age. The churches supported Graham because they felt he was a "team player," not seeking support for his own cause. Instead he directed his converts to the churches and helped the churches grow.

Library of Congress

Billy Graham Archives

Through the work of Dwight L. Moody (1837-1899), top; Billy Sunday (1862-1935), middle; Billy Graham (b. 1918), bottom; and others; revivalism has continued as an important part of American church life.

Billy Graham Center

51

V Beyond Congregational Worship

18 Foreign Missions

In the 1800s many Christians sent missionaries to lands where Christianity was unknown. In this century, some missionaries have changed their emphasis from church-building and preaching to understanding others' faith and culture and to providing education and medical help.

The Christians of Typical City are not content with being the only Christians in the world. They are aware of other Christians in other American places. And they want to share their faith with people in other nations as well.

Christianity moved from its beginnings in Jerusalem to the whole "known world" in a generation or two. Not much is known as to exactly how it spread in the second and third century. But by the end of this period Christianity was ready to become the official religion of the Roman Empire. All through the centuries to follow, through the Middle Ages, missionaries went on their own or with conquerors to seek new victories for Christ. A king would be baptized and his people would follow.

In the age of exploration, the 1500s and 1600s, missionaries came with Columbus's successors to bring Catholicism to America. At the same time men like Francis Xavier went to Asia with the Gospel, trying to baptize and convert people. Some Protestants who came to America wanted to carry on a mission to the Native Americans.

The great age of modern missions, however, came early in the nineteenth century. Ships from England, Europe, and America were taking merchants to India, other parts of Asia, and Africa. Never before was it so easy to send missionaries as in that age of expansion. Who would go?

All of a sudden, men and women in England caught the fever of missions. They founded great societies to send evangelizers. These people preached, converted natives, built hospitals, founded schools. Early in the nineteenth century young men at some of the Protestant colleges of New England, schools like Williams and Amherst, or the new theological seminary

52

at Andover, Massachusetts, banded together. The Sandwich (Hawaiian) Islands had been discovered, and some Hawaiians had come to America. Soon Americans sent people to Hawaii.

The missionary movement was shaped by people who became heroes to many back home. The best known of these in the first generation was Adoniram Judson. In 1810 he offered to go to Burma as a missionary. He and his wife, Ann, faced hard times with Burmese Buddhists. As Burmese in conflict with England and thus with people from the Christian world, the Buddhists did not like his faith. Judson was imprisoned. Letters he sent back helped inspire more support of missions by Americans.

He needed their encouragement because he made few converts and was often in very low spirits. His example helped buoy the spirits of missionaries who went elsewhere with more success.

By the end of the nineteenth century Americans made up much of the world mission force. The stories of missionaries, by mail or when they came home on furlough, inspired others with a vision of Christian courage and love.

At the turn of the century American missions were graced by a tireless traveler, John R. Mott. A Methodist student, he considered colleges to be the battleground for the minds and hearts of the young. So he built up a stu-

While a prisoner on a forced march through the Burmese jungle, foreign missionary Adoniram Judson accepts cloth to wrap his torn feet.

53

John R. Mott, 1865-1955
Tireless Supporter of Christian Missions

dent missionary movement, first in America and then around the world. Someone estimated that he traveled 1.75 million miles—before the jet airplane was invented. His diaries and letters suggest he was seasick most of those miles.

Despite his own hardships, Mott never lost his energy or zeal. He wanted students, lay people, and church leaders to come together so that the world would know Christ. Mott did so much for Christian and religious understanding that nonbelievers also caught a vision of concord. For his efforts this man of God received the Nobel Peace Prize in 1946.

In recent decades, however, many Christians have had second thoughts about the old way of doing missionary work. They have not disbanded the organizations to send people, but not all are so ready to land on Muslims, Hindus, Buddhists, or Jews, and try to replace their faith and culture with that of the West. Instead of converting, they converse and try to understand. Instead of building chapels, they concentrate on hospitals.

To the more conservative and evangelistic church bodies, this policy seems wrong and cruel. They believe that unreached people who never come to Christ cannot go to heaven and will go to hell. Therefore the most loving thing to do is to send missionaries to get them out of heathenism or paganism.

Enthusiastic Pentecostal or "Spirit" movements originating in America have broken out in Latin America and Africa, where they are the fastest growing Christian force. So rapidly are these churches growing that they have often been able to send the missionaries home. They are "younger churches," with indigenous or native clergy. Soon there may be more Christians in the southern hemisphere than in the northern.

Churches in Typical City are likely to have displays showing where "their" missionaries are. Some congregations sponsor a number of missionaries. Catholics, for instance, support religious orders who work among non-Christian people. Visiting missionaries bring some vision of the world church to people who will never leave home. The motives and programs vary, but all these Christians believe that somehow the circle of those who believe must grow, both in numbers and in quality of faith and love. ●

American Christians support work in the name of Christ in all parts of the world.

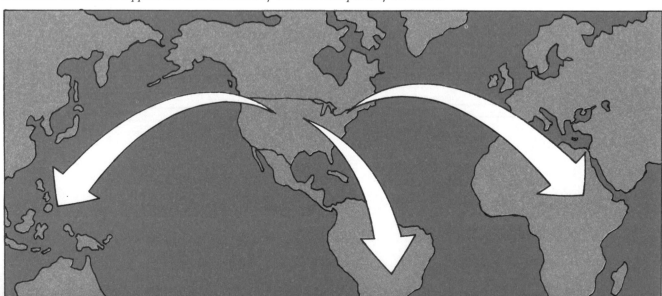

19 Church Education

Children who worked in factories in the 1800s did not have a chance to go to school, but some of them learned to read and write in Sunday school, and studied the Bible at the same time.

In order to teach young people Christian faith and traditions, churches in the United States support many educational agencies. Among these are Sunday schools, parochial schools, and church-related colleges.

The visitor to Typical City will pass quite a number of public schools and perhaps a state college or university. They are not the only educational institutions in town. Down the block may be a Luther College or a Calvin College, or even a University of Notre Dame. Next door to Catholic churches there will often be Catholic schools, next to Lutheran churches, Lutheran schools; as a part of synagogues there may well be Jewish schools.

Parents have to see that their children are nurtured in faith. Once upon a time this was easy to do. Everyone who grew up in Spain was Catholic; in Sweden, Lutheran; in a European ghetto, Jewish. (Ghetto was the name given to the separate part of a city where Jews had to live.) You never learned to know that there were religions other than your own, and you were not really free to leave the religious house of your parents. They automatically passed on to you the stories of your faith.

Today all is different. Public schools do not support particular faiths. Television beams signals into homes without regard for the faith of those who are there. Young people go off to college, military service, or work, meeting people of different backgrounds. Sometimes they marry persons of different faiths.

When church leaders caught on to the new situation—one that began with religious freedom two centuries ago—they began to invent new kinds of agencies to educate the young, to help pass on the faith to children.

In England and America the most popular invention was the Sunday school. An English churchman, Robert Raikes, began developing this kind of school after 1786, and it was soon imported to America. Many children at that time worked in factories and did not attend school. Those early Sunday schools taught children how to read and write, using the Bible as the main text book. Originally an all-day-long affair, Sunday school today has come to be an hour-long event in most Protestant churches.

Sunday school combines biblical stories, worship, crafts, and visual aids—all designed to help give children the beginnings of what they need to know about their faith. Often the home fails to do this.

The second great modern agency for educating is the parochial or Christian day school. Many of these were started by Catholics in the nineteenth century, when public schools frequently were institutions that supported Protestantism. During the school day, children often read from the Protestant King James Version of the Bible. History lessons sometimes included statements against the pope and the Roman Catholic Church. Catholics were then too few in number to make changes in the public schools, so they started their own schools. Soon Lutherans, Christian Reformed (Dutch), Seventh-day Adventists, and, in recent times, many fundamentalist Christians followed the example.

Marilyn Larson

American churches have often founded colleges. Many of these colleges keep their church ties, although some no longer have church connections. A typical church college campus is shown above.

Parochial schools are paid for entirely by the families or churches of those who attend them. Children learn all the regular subjects plus religion in an atmosphere where teachers can speak freely about their own faith. Many synagogues also have schools, because Jews need to learn Hebrew to participate in their worship and understand their tradition.

A third form of religious education is the church-related college. Long before the American Revolution, Congregationalists started Harvard and Yale colleges. Other denominations copied these plans. As people came to the frontier, revivalists often started colleges to train more ministers. From the first they also taught language, history, and other subjects, and fine universities were born. Many church colleges later dropped their church ties, but

hundreds of good schools have kept them. These schools also teach all subjects, but they are likely to have a major chapel, a religion department, and the chance for the outlook of faith to shine through all that goes on.

Typical City may also have a seminary, where people study to be priests, ministers, or rabbis. After graduating from college, people attend these schools to learn more about faith and how to minister to others.

Someone has said that in religion it is not what you know but Who you know that matters. Yet knowing Who God is also leads people to be curious about what God has meant and how to serve God. For that, there has to be religious education, and the city hums with its agencies.

As one of the symbols of the gifts of life brought to the altar, a baby from Zimbabwe is presented to Philip Potter, leader of the World Council of Churches, at the opening worship of the 1983 World Council Assembly in Vancouver, British Columbia, Canada.

20 Councils of Churches

Many different denominations work together in the World Council of Churches, and the National Council of Churches, and state councils, and local councils of churches.

One way in which churches are connected does not follow the lines of denominations—First Baptist, Second Baptist, and the like. Instead they cross these lines between church bodies. American churches have also formed councils or federations of churches. Usually you will not see these councils mentioned on the signs in front of churches. They are not highly visible in office buildings in Typical City.

The largest of these agencies is the World Council of Churches, founded in 1948 with the support of most mainline American Protestants. Orthodox Churches also belong to it, but Roman Catholics on one hand and fundamentalists on another do not. The World Council of Churches exists to promote Christian unity. It has also helped with relief in the midst of wars, with medical aid and food for displaced persons and the poor. Because so many of its members are from the Third World, and thus are people who represent concerns and policies different from those most Americans cherish, not all members of American churches speak well of this Council. Still, they recognize that it provides a way for them to work with people who are in circumstances very different from theirs.

Similarly there is in the United States a National Council of Churches, founded in 1950 to replace an older Federal Council of Churches, which was begun in 1908. This Council attracts Protestant and Orthodox church bodies of moderate to liberal persuasion. The Council produced the Revised Standard Version of the Bible. It also carries on work among migrants. It helped bring about civil rights laws which have changed race relations in America. The National Council, too, is often controversial.

Then there are state and local councils of churches. Interchurch councils often hold joint worship programs, for example, on Thanksgiving Day. They may help with community services, Christmas tree lightings, Memorial Day services, and the like. It may be up to them to advertise the role of religion in life, using radio or television. These local councils often succeed in doing big things with small budgets. They can sense needs that a local church cannot handle or perhaps even see—because the church is located in a suburb, or a ghetto.

What about the conservative Protestants who believe that they will compromise their faith if they worship and work too closely with mainline Protestants, Orthodox, or Catholics? They have organized groups like the National Association of Evangelicals, started in 1942. They also formed local evangelical coalitions. Once upon

The Revised Standard Version, one of the most used of modern Bible translations, was produced by the National Council of Churches.

a time these evangelicals refused to cooperate with anyone else. In recent years they have been friendlier to Catholics and Jews and on certain causes they link up with more liberal Protestants. It often happens that people in Typical City who cannot agree on doctrine can unite their efforts to help migrant workers, victims of disaster, and others in need.

People of different traditions worshiping together witness to the breadth of the Church.

VI
Heirs of the Frontier

21 The United Methodists

United Methodism is America's third largest church. Efficient organization has helped its rapid growth. People responded to the call to experience a "warmed heart," to become holy, and then to spread holiness. Bishop Francis Asbury was a strong early leader.

John Wesley, 1703-1791
Founder of the Methodist Church

This map shows regions in the United States where the majority of church members are Methodists.

Bishop Francis Asbury, American Methodist bishop and leader, developed the art of circuit riding and traveled thousands of miles visiting tiny frontier settlements.

The United Methodist Church will have one of the larger churches and some smaller ones in almost any city. One out of every 10 American church members belongs to this, America's third largest church body.

Methodists belong to the mainline of Protestantism. Most white Methodists are in the United Methodist Church. This was formed by a merger first, in 1939, of northern and southern bodies and then, in 1968, by linking with the smaller Evangelical United Brethren, a Methodist-type group with German-speaking roots.

Methodism began with a kind of three-part approach, all parts of which live on in this church today. First, founder John Wesley wanted his followers to experience the "warmed heart," and he preached to rouse their emotions. He felt that the Church of England in the mid-eighteenth century was too staid and that its members were passive and relaxed. Second, the Methodists were and are organizational geniuses. They invented intricate small groups called "classes," and orderly forms of government. Third, Methodists have always been world-changers. Wesley preached "perfection." Christians were to become holy themselves and then to spread holiness.

After the Revolutionary War, at Christmas in 1784, Lovely Lane Church in Baltimore welcomed a gathering of Methodists who organized an American branch. Twenty years later, Methodists were competing with the Baptists to be the largest church in the new United States. How and why were they so successful? The career of pioneer Bishop Francis Asbury (1745-1816) helps answer this. Asbury, the greatest American Methodist, was a black-

Methodism's orderly form of church government, here suggested by the lists and charts of this planning group, furthered its rapid growth in the United States. Its great appeal, however, is the message that God is loving and that people are capable of great things in the world.

ens of times he crossed what he called his "Alps," the Appalachian Mountains. His *Journals* record thousands of miles of painful travel. Asbury was afflicted with every sort of misery from bad teeth to arthritis, but he pressed on.

Asbury had no time for the love of a wife. He regretted the fact that some of his itinerant preachers, circuit riders, had what he called "darlings" back home. To him a marriage carriage looked like a hearse.

Asbury had little money and little use for it. As a circuit rider, he slept in frontier cabins, often on rude beds with two or three other traveling men. His clothes were often wet, always ill-fitting, usually well-worn. Yet he always found energy for another of his 16,500 sermons. Under Asbury's governance, over 4,000 other Methodist preachers went forth across the mountains through the border states and beyond.

Asbury would fire up the people with calls to spontaneous conversion. Like many another Methodist, however, he was also a disciplined man who, he said, always preached "Order! Order!" the second time he came around. The Methodist Church *was* ordered. Its competitors thought it was too dominated from above by church executives, too rigid. Yet the common people loved this form of Christianity. Asbury's message, like Wesley's, stressed that God was a God of love and that humans were capable of great things in the name of God.

Methodists have been great builders of churches. Today almost 40,000 congregations serve about 10 million members. These believers have always thought God wanted them to reform the world and spread justice in it. In 1908 they produced a Social Creed, which called for a kind of progressive solution to the world's evils. Methodists helped lead the long temperance battle that finally led in 1920 to prohibition of alcoholic beverages in the United States. They believed drunkenness was sinful. Alcohol produced social problems for families of victims who used it too freely and spent too much money on it. At its best, it is Methodist preaching of the message of Christian holiness and perfection that has given life to its congregations. When Methodists get bogged down, tired, burdened by their own organization, they seek renewal through the message of God's love in Christ, God's call for them to spread scriptural holiness throughout the land. ●

smith and lay preacher in England. He came to America in 1771. Three years later he became a "superintendent," the term then used for bishop. Asbury was loyal to Methodism, but he did not believe he had to take orders from Wesley, who he thought had misunderstood America.

Asbury quickly developed the art of "circuit riding," making many stops in tiny frontier settlements. At each he performed marriages and baptisms, called for the conversion of people, and organized congregations. Nightly he would saddle his horse and make off for another cluster of people in the wilderness. Doz-

22 The Southern Baptists

The Southern Baptist denomination is America's largest Protestant church. Its priorities are reaching out to unchurched people and biblical preaching.

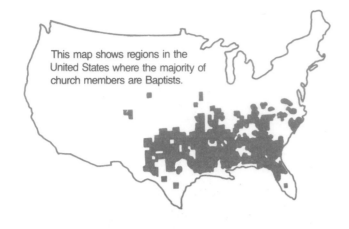

This map shows regions in the United States where the majority of church members are Baptists.

Evangelist Billy Graham, above, and President Jimmy Carter, below, are among well-known Southern Baptists of the 1970s and '80s.

The Southern Baptists deserve separate treatment as the most successful of the frontier denominations which moved southwest across the mountains early in the nineteenth century. The Southern Baptists were guided by no single person's vision. This is the case in part because they are in many ways so independent-minded, so strongly congregational. But even without a dominant evangelist, missionary, planner, bureaucrat, or theologian, the Baptists devised a package of Christianity that appealed to frontier settlers and city folk alike.

Today it is not hard to find Southern Baptists nearby. This is the case no matter whether our Typical City is in the South, where this 13-million member denomination has its heartland, or in the North. Southern Baptists, busy winning converts in the Sunbelt in a time of population growth, have also discovered a hunger for their approach in the North. They try to reach the forty percent of America which is unchurched and work among underchurched populations like the Hispanic people. Some northern Baptists, and other Christians who found their previous church life too relaxed, prefer the biblical firmness and general conservatism of most Southern Baptists.

The visitor from abroad has little trouble recognizing or feeling at home with Southern Baptist worship if he or she has watched television. The church is likely to be more like an auditorium than a cathedral or chapel for liturgy. Evangelist Billy Graham and many lesser lights have spread its style. There is a homey, folksy atmosphere of friendliness and informal acceptance. The hymns are for the most part from the "Gospel hymn" or "soul song" tradition, many of them written originally for use in revival meetings. Many members know these hymns from memory. Sermons are strongly biblical messages, and there are emphatic moral appeals along with preaching of the gospel of Jesus Christ. Through the years, however, some churches have grown ever more formal, their members revealing taste for the art, music, and liturgy of the ages. For all the apparent unity that conservatism should bring, there are controversies. Southern Baptists were divided from the first. They fought over the understanding of God's initiative and power alongside human will and response. Some Baptists were "antimission." They believed the church should have no agencies which work for conversion since

Baptism by immersion—sometimes in a stream or river—is customary among Baptists.

God was the only converter. The missionary people generally won out. "Landmark" Baptists believed that only Baptists made up the true church. A creedless church by definition, in 1925 the Convention forged a conservative Baptist Faith and Message to describe its normal expression. Some have used it as a creed.

Baptists could claim to be very democratic. A local church could start out on its own, while the Methodist competitor had to wait for a circuit rider and was governed by superintendents and bishops.

The Southern Baptist Convention was born in 1845 over fights between northern and southern states about the slavery issue. In the decades following, a south-wide organization formed. The seminaries grew and very gradually became more and more like seminaries of other denominations. Baptist prosperity and fame have led to conflict. Ultra-traditional Baptists are afraid that in many churches new ideas are creeping in, ideas that might subvert the never official but widely believed fundamentalist teaching that the Bible is an accu-

rate authority even in matters of science and history. "God cannot lie."

The biblical conservatism needed to defend slavery on literal grounds, along with a climate of defensiveness against the liberal North, led southern people to use their churches to resist modern ideas. It was not until the South turned urban and cosmopolitan, after World War II, that the controversies erupted there. The Convention is today quite divided with a slight but highly organized majority in the fundamentalist-leaning camp.

It is hard to describe the Southern Baptists, so large and varied is their denomination. More and more its clergy are gaining positions of influence in the United States. People who once looked down on it as "the church of the southern poor" now have seen it represented by Billy Graham, President Jimmy Carter, and the Christian television networks. They have come to envy it as a smoothly-operating and effective denomination that embodies many of the extremes that live on in American religious life. ●

23 The Disciples of Christ

Unlike Christians in many other Protestant churches, the Disciples of Christ celebrate Holy Communion every week.

The Disciples of Christ, or Christian Church, was founded in America in 1827. Disciples try to worship exactly as New Testament Christians did. Congregations are very independent, and there are now several church bodies in this family.

Next to the Methodists in the west end of Typical City and the Baptists in the southwest, is an example of an American-born denomination. The sign out front reads Christian Church (Disciples of Christ). This group was not on the scene until the nineteenth century. It grew in numbers chiefly because of its success as a third (along with the Baptists and Methodists) revivalist denomination on the frontier. Today 37 out of 1,000 American church members are "Christian (Campbellite)." They belong to the Disciples of Christ or other clusters of churches that grew up as the result of the work of Thomas Campbell (1763-1854) and his more noted son, Alexander (1788-1866).

The Campbells' vision, then, is important for anyone who wants to understand this American-born denomination. Thomas Campbell migrated to America from Scotland in 1807. A vigorous enemy of sects and schisms, Campbell thought he had a clue to overcoming squabbles in his own Presbyterian Church and other denominations. In 1809 he joined with others to form the Christian Association of Washington, Pennsylvania. They announced that they were completely faithful to the New Testament alone. No mere traditions of the later church should

The Disciples of Christ model their weekly Communion after the example, shown above, of the early Christians.

influence them. Where the Scriptures speak, said Campbell, we speak; where the Scriptures are silent, we are silent.

Soon Thomas passed his mantle on to his better-known son Alexander, who joined a "Christian Association" in 1812. Brought up Presbyterian, Campbell came to believe in the Baptist form of baptizing adults by immersion. Straddling the two groups was difficult, he soon learned. This was a sign to him that denominationalism was evil. In 1827 Campbell became the leader of what he called the Disciples of Christ, but which his enemies insisted on calling "the Campbellites." This was not to be a denomination or a sect, but a movement which he hoped all right-thinking Christians would join.

For a man who was seeking unity, Campbell was a very argumentative person. He debated the Presbyterians and Baptists, in whose company he had grown up, just as he argued with Catholic bishops, freethinkers like Robert Owen, and any or all comers. Since many of his converts came from Baptist churches, considerable competition and envy developed on the frontier. Campbell helped merge his movement in 1832 with Warren Barton Stone's "the Christian Connection," another example of primitive Christianity on the frontier. Despite the distaste of Campbell and Stone for denominations, they became, against their will, pioneers in still another denomination.

The worshiper at a Disciples of Christ (Christian) Church in the North today will find it very much a member of mainline Protestantism. Church architecture ranges all the way from meeting-hall types to more ornate Gothic styles, but the majority of church buildings are

*Alexander Campbell, 1788-1866
Founder with his father, Thomas, of
the Disciples of Christ*

*This old photograph shows
Alexander late in life, with his
second wife.*

quite simple and unadorned. The denomination's general social outlook will be on the moderate to liberal side. While members expect much of the sermon, Disciples of Christ have also long been distinctive among Protestants because of their practice of a weekly Holy Communion. They have this meal every Sunday because they believe the early Christians did. They want to follow the example of the disciples quite literally. For many years, because the New Testament made no mention of organ accompaniment, many Campbellite churches opposed the use of organs.

At the turn of the century some of the northern Disciples helped produce the liberal and modernist movements in Protestant theology. The mainline Disciples of Christ moved into the ecumenical movement, taking liberal social stands and allowing for critical readings of the Bible. The right wing, some of whom may have remained in the main body and some of whom were always a part of the more fiercely congregational bodies, moved further rightward. When the Disciples "restructured" in 1968 so that they became a little more like other denominations, over 2,300 congregations withdrew from the membership roster in protest.

Most of the fundamentalist "Campbellites" have really tried hard not to be a denomination, something that is difficult to do in America. They are found mainly in two national bodies, each with over a million members. But they insist that they are fellowships without headquarters. They have many Bible colleges. They support missionaries, and even a publishing house. But they insist that they have no president, bishop, or bureaucracy to limit local congregations. This makes counting membership difficult, but in the Southwest the Churches of Christ, as one group is known, make up one of the fastest-growing Protestant churches in America.

Members of these groups are more literal in interpreting the Bible than are many members of the Disciples. They practice footwashing, and they also join their more liberal partners in weekly observance of the Lord's Supper in the form of an open Communion. To the observer, they look very much like other fundamentalists. Their sermons will accent the idea of an inerrant Bible, full of "Thus saith the Lord's." Like the Disciples of Christ, they try to keep the idea of Christian simplicity alive in a complex age.

24 The Latter-Day Saints, or Mormons

The Church of Jesus Christ of Latter-Day Saints was founded by Joseph Smith about 1830. In 1847, Brigham Young took a large group to Utah, now a Mormon base and stronghold. For this church, Smith's *Book of Mormon* stands with the Bible as an authority. For this reason, many Christians distrust the Mormons.

Joseph Smith, 1805-1844
Founder of the Church of Jesus Christ
of Latter-Day Saints

One of the most fascinating of all churches in America, a mystery to the outsiders whom its members call gentiles, is the Church of Jesus Christ of Latter-Day Saints. The public knows its members as Mormons, named after *The Book of Mormon,* its sacred book. Upstate New Yorker Joseph Smith (1805-1844), the Mormon prophet, claimed to have a revelation which tied the plan of God not only to ancient Israel and the times of Jesus, but to the American scene itself. The book he propagated included the American Indians and blacks as part of its plot.

Mormons affirmed Jesus, but they interpreted him so differently that they were repudiated by other Christians, who have not regarded them as a true Christian church. To most Christians, the Mormon belief that humans are, in a sense, growing into godhood or godhead, is a mark of pantheism.

Whatever their Christian status, the Mormons prosper. In 1950 there were perhaps a million in America; today 30 out of every 1,000 United States church members are Mormons. The church claims almost 3 million members in over 7,000 local gatherings. Since almost all young males spend two years recruiting, many of them overseas, worldwide growth is astonishing. Since all members tithe, the church is well off.

The roots of the Mormon vision are easy to trace. To his critics, in the 1830s as today, Joseph Smith seemed to be a fake. To his followers he was a true prophet of God, selected to receive a long-hidden revelation. Born in Vermont, he came with his parents to a farm in

This map shows regions in the United States where the majority of church members are Mormons.

Many Mormons give two years of their life to missionary work. Here a Mormon offers to share his faith with a non-Mormon.

New York. In the 1820s, there were many revivals in that region. Smith said later that he was confused by the many competing claims of the evangelists and asked for divine guidance.

The young man was given a series of visions. At the time many New Yorkers were digging to find buried treasure. Smith, digging on Hill Cumorah, found golden plates to translate, using two mysterious "seer" stones, he said. In 1830 he published his *Book of Mormon*. Smith felt called to start a new kingdom, one built on the idea of economic cooperation. Soon he had followers who wanted to help him spread his community. Smith moved the group to Ohio, to Missouri, and then to Illinois. About this time it became public that Smith claimed a revelation that made polygamy, the holding of several wives, permissible. This fact, along with his dream of a separate kingdom, scandalized the "gentiles." In 1844 in a mob scene at a jail in Carthage, Illinois, he was shot. A greater organizer, Brigham Young (1801-1877), then took over and led the group to Utah, which became the Mormon kingdom and stronghold. Another Mormon group, called the Reorganized Church of Latter-Day Saints, its base in Independence, Missouri, never practiced polygamy. It stayed closer to orthodox Christianity but never grew as large as the main body of Mormons.

In order to gain statehood for Utah, which they did in 1896, the main group of Mormons had to drop the practice of polygamy. Statehood brought an end to hostilities between the Mormons and the rest of the United States. Through the years the church has become ever more visible as a very patriotic nationalist group. The frugality and ambition of members, their reputation for wholesome family life, and their care for each other's welfare has won Mormons a better reputation among the millions of other Americans who still think the Mormon religion is based upon a fraud.

A typical American city does not have one of the great Mormon Temples. Most are where the Mormon population long dominated, as in Utah, and parts of Idaho, California, and Hawaii.

The Temples are not the local community's house of worship. Only Saints in good standing can ever enter these sacred buildings. They are used for distinctive Mormon practices such as "baptism for the dead" and "celestial marriages," which seal partners for all eternity. Baptism for the dead makes possible a new saving act for those who have already died. Mormons therefore are intense genealogists. They have collected family trees which include names of over a billion people.

Conservative, prosperous, and familial, the Mormons seem to have a great future. They demand strong commitment from their members and never tire of efforts to convert others. ●

In 1848 a flock of sea gulls in Utah devoured a horde of grasshoppers who were devastating the Mormons' crops. This providential incident is still commemorated among the Mormons.

VII
Black
Denominations

25 The Black Baptists

Religious News Service

Martin Luther King, Jr., 1929-1968
Black Baptist Minister

Baptists are the largest church among black people, and its preachers are often leaders in black communities. The best-known modern leader among black Baptists was Martin Luther King, Jr., who led the civil rights movement.

One of the largest churches in Typical City will be a black Baptist church. Once upon a time its huge sanctuary belonged to a largely white congregation; its members moved to the suburbs and left the building behind. In the poorer, segregated black neighborhoods, Baptist churches predominate. Black Baptist churches, whether meeting in large sanctuaries or modest storefronts, serve as islands of stability in the slums as well as places of power in middle-class communities. They are centers of hope and celebration where young people develop their

Secretly and at great risk, black slaves learned to read and preach and formed their own churches.

talents and older people express them. People there overcome loneliness and anonymity and have their spiritual needs met. The congregation in these churches believes God is close to them.

The majority of black Christians is Baptist because in the era of slavery Negroes lived chiefly in the deep South where Baptist churches dominated. While many of the well-off slaveholders were Presbyterian, Methodist, or Episcopal, some of the most motivated preachers among the slaves were Baptists. Owners often discouraged slaves from becoming preachers.

They didn't permit them to learn to read or write, because such abilities brought power and led slaves to yearn for freedom. Reading the Bible was especially dangerous, because blacks read the story of Moses as their own story, and they looked for exodus, liberation, and a promised land.

Despite all the discouragements, however, blacks did learn to read and to preach. When the slaveowners' backs were turned, slaves formed their own churches. Sometimes there would also be black freemen in the South. Blacks adopted and then adapted the Baptist faith to

Peaceful demonstrations led by King inspired both black and white Americans to work for civil rights.

We know that even before the Revolution there was a black Baptist church at Silver Bluff in South Carolina. Since good records are not available, we cannot be sure how many others there were. Black churches could not connect with each other in the early South. The first record of an association of black Baptist churches dates from Ohio in 1836. Not until 1880, fifteen years after the Civil War, were there enough free and ready blacks who could organize a mission enterprise.

Two black denominations are very large. The National Baptist Convention, USA, Inc.—while they are too dispersed to come up with accurate statistics—claims well over 5 million members in 26,000 churches. This would make it the third largest Prostestant church in America. The National Baptist Convention of America also thrives, claiming 2.7 million people in over 11,000 churches. Both carry on mission work in Africa.

By far the best-known black Baptist in American history has been Martin Luther King, Jr., (1929-1968), son of an Atlanta minister. He studied in black institutions in Atlanta and then pursued doctoral work and graduated with a Ph.D. from Boston University. As a minister in Montgomery, Alabama, and then at his home church in Atlanta, he attracted national attention. To the folks in the pew, he was cut from his father's mold. He was serious, biblically minded, concerned about injustice, and hopeful about what God and the people together might do. Black Christians did not see King as in any way departing from the black Baptist tradition. But the largely white culture, which did not know that tradition, was not sure how to explain King's spiritual roots.

The young minister became head of the Southern Christian Leadership Conference, which he led from 1957 until his murder in 1968. During those years, King tried to revive the Social Gospel, blend it with black themes, and awaken the conscience of America. His sermons, rallies, writings, and letters from jail were modern "epistles" of an apostle. He was capable of leading followers in peaceful demonstrations which often brought out the violence of the people in power. After these confrontations many Americans were inspired to find a conscience and a motive for resolving issues of civil rights. ●

their purposes. Many of them welcomed the spontaneity of Baptist faith. They liked the accent on conversion, on being "born again," on having God give them a new start and the promise of liberation. The songs white Baptists sang were not stiff and formal. The blacks took them over, or came up with their own counterpart, Negro spirituals, as they came to be called. Each individual church was free to do things its own way.

26 The Black Methodists

Black Methodism, founded in the early 1800s, is an important agency for the development of black leadership. Its founder was Richard Allen, a former slave.

White Methodists at St. George's Church in Philadelphia refused to let Richard Allen and other blacks sit with white members.

Down the block from the large black Baptist congregation in Typical City is one with Methodist connections. There are two large black Methodist national groups, each with about 6,000 local churches. The African Methodist Episcopal Church claims over 2 million members and the African Methodist Episcopal Zion Church over 1.3 million. The slight difference in their names suggests, quite properly, that they are much like each other.

The pioneering vision that shaped black Methodism came to Richard Allen (1760-1831).

Born a slave, he purchased his liberty at age twenty-one. Well aware of the problems of being a black in America, Allen was determined to get beyond those problems. The warm sermons of Methodist traveling preachers confirmed him in faith, and he made heroes of them. He would, he decided, join other Methodists in preaching and saving souls—and organizing Methodism.

Only one problem stood between him and his dreams: He was black. This meant limited opportunity in the church and the need to make a living for his family by doing odd jobs. In

After the confrontation in St. George's Church, Richard Allen and his friends founded Bethel Methodist Church, the "mother church" of Black Methodism, in 1794.
The old drawing below shows the church as it was rebuilt in 1805.

BETHEL AFRICAN METHODIST EPISCOPAL CHURCH, PHILADᵃ
Founded in 1744 by the Revᵈ Richard Allen, Bishop of the First African Methodist Episcopal Church in the United States. ___ Rebuilt in 1805.
Drawn on Stone by W.L.Breton. Philadᵃ July 1829   Kennedy & Lucas' Lithogra

Philadelphia, St. George's Methodist Church provided him with a base. He got along well in that humanitarian-minded city with its generous congregations. Yet there was not sufficient hospitality. The whites at St. George's kept to the strict conventions of the day and wanted to keep the races apart. This led to a confrontation.

As Allen told it years later, perhaps changing some details, he, Absalom Jones, who became the first black Episcopal priest in America, and other blacks were worshiping in St. George's. Some white trustees insisted that they move to the gallery, where they believed the blacks should be confined. Jones later remembered that he asked the trustee to wait until the prayer ended. "No, you must get up now, or I will call for aid and force you away." Again Jones refused. The trustee motioned for help to grab and remove the blacks just as the prayer ended. Allen and his company then marched out: "They were no more plagued with us in the church."

After a few years of worship wherever they could find quarters, Allen and friends helped found Bethel Church, known as the mother church of black Methodism. Francis Asbury showed his respect by coming to dedicate it. The blacks virtually had to pay for the church twice to gain the title, but eventually it became theirs, the first of many buildings of black Methodists.

Allen was a Methodist as much as he was a black. He loved the order of his church and the opportunities it provided. He was a very ambitious man, and a competitive leader, James Varick, resenting Allen's style, established the African Methodist Episcopal Zion Church on a parallel track.

In 1816 some well-meaning whites helped establish Liberia in Africa as a refuge for freed slaves. The American Colonization Society, as they called their movement, wanted Allen to lend his name to strengthen the society's reputation. He refused to give his support, denouncing the society. Allen and his fellow Methodists felt strongly that America was now their land as much as anyone else's, even though their ancestors had not wanted to come to here. As one black of the times said: "They had watered it with their tears and fertilized it with their blood."

During the years of slavery the A.M.E. and A.M.E. Zion churches grew along with the rest of Methodism. At the close of the Civil War they competed almost ruthlessly with each other and with a black branch of the largely white Methodist Church. Whites played the three churches off against each other. Sometimes rival Methodist black groups even burned each other's little churches. But these were only slightly more flagrant forms of the competition that went on in most of the churches of the time.

Eventually the organizations stabilized and became, along with the black Baptist churches, the main agencies of developing black leadership. Some of these talents stayed in the church and some of them moved on. W. E. Burghardt Du Bois (1868-1963) was a Harvard-educated Negro leader who later turned against religion and became a Communist. At the beginning of the twentieth century he spoke of black Methodism as the most effective organization in American Negro history. ●

Black Methodism has been important in the development of black leaders.

VIII
Heirs of Continental Establishments

27 The Lutherans

Lutherans came to America from Europe after American churches of English origin were already well established. Lutherans faced the problem of deciding how Americanized they wanted to be. Like founder Martin Luther, Lutherans today emphasize God's grace and forgiveness.

Martin Luther, 1483-1546
Founder of the Lutheran Church

This map shows regions in the United States where the majority of church members are Lutherans.

Not quite downtown in symbolic Typical City is the Lutheran church. The downtowners were people whose ancestors came from the British Isles. The Lutherans, most of whom arrived from Germany and Scandinavia, migrated a little later. Because they spoke a foreign language and came to a scene that was already churched, they did not so readily enter the religious mainstream. Now, more Americans can trace their roots to Germany than to any other nation. But for a long time, even long after the

Revolution, a faith transplanted from the European continent was still at a disadvantage in an English-speaking country.

This did not mean that Lutheranism has not prospered in America. When the nation was born, Lutherans, with 240 churches, were the fifth largest denominational group in the colonies. Today it is the fourth largest cluster; 6 out of every 100 American church members are Lutheran. About 9 million citizens are members of the oldest and largest of the world's Protestant families.

While Lutherans have not played a large part in shaping the public life of the nation, they have cherished their church life. Theirs is the church of greats like composer Johann Sebastian Bach. Lutheran worship, marked by classic hymns or "chorales," focuses on "the ministry of word and sacrament." Therefore their buildings give about equal attention to the pulpit, the altar, and the baptismal font. Lutheran preaching focuses on the forgiveness of sins, the theme that meant so much to Martin Luther, the German monk who left the Roman Catholic Church in the sixteenth century. At the same time, as conservative reformers, the early Lutherans kept their version of the Catholic mass or Eucharist. Lutheran books used for worship call for Holy Communion as the normal service every Sunday, though some congregations commune only monthly.

Some Lutherans, notably those of Missouri and Wisconsin synods, sponsor parish schools much like Catholic schools. While Lutherans have been less involved than many other Christians in taking stands on issues of social justice, they have put energies into works of charity, seeking, in Luther's terms, to make "faith active in love."

Lutherans came in the colonial period, but their greatest surge came toward the middle of the nineteenth century as a crowded Europe sent its overflow to seize American opportunities. Some of the newcomers had resisted efforts by the state churches of northern Europe to control their faith life. So such immigrants were resistant to the lures of the American religious environment, since they wanted no entanglements or pressures in their churches.

Lutheranism long faced the problem of deciding how "Americanized" it wanted to be. Two leaders with competing visions represent the main choices. Samuel Simon Schmucker (1799-

Johann Sebastian Bach, 1685-1750
Great Lutheran Composer

1873), professor at the Gettysburg, Pennsylvania, Seminary from 1826 to 1864, was known as an Americanizer. He organized eastern Lutherans, seeking to make them as much like the rest of American Protestants as possible. His basic Lutheranism was never in doubt. Schmucker simply thought his church would prosper if it seemed less foreign. In 1838 he wrote a "Fraternal Appeal to the American Churches" to unite.

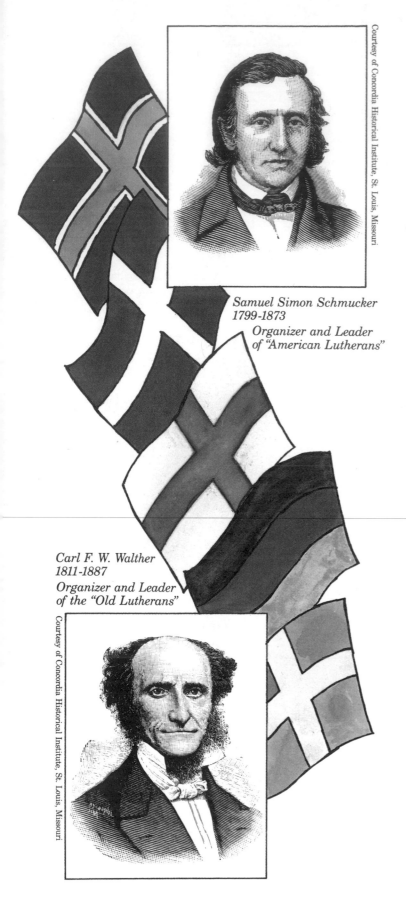

*Samuel Simon Schmucker
1799-1873*

*Organizer and Leader
of "American Lutherans"*

*Carl F. W. Walther
1811-1887*

*Organizer and Leader
of the "Old Lutherans"*

*Most Lutheran immigrants to the United States came
from the countries represented by the flags in this
picture. From the top, they are: Norway, Sweden,
Finland, Germany, and Denmark.*

Schmucker's "American Lutherans," however, soon met opposition from the frontier German "Old Lutherans," who came toward mid-century and after. Their leader was a staunch Saxon, Carl F. W. Walther (1811-1887), a University of Leipzig graduate who was the leader at the Missouri Synod's Concordia Seminary from 1850 to 1887 and was for years president of the synod itself. Almost chinless, bewhiskered, scowling, Walther used the German-language magazine *Der Lutheraner* to rally the new people as they came off the boats. Walther lived spiritually back in the seventeenth century, the "good old days" when he thought doctrine had been pure. He wanted his fellow believers to avoid "Unionism" with other Protestants and even with Lutherans of Schmucker's Americanized type. Walther helped give the new immigrants a strong identity and pride in the truth they held. He implied that only they and those in perfect agreement with them made up "the true visible church on earth."

Lutheranism was salted with many other kinds of movements. Among these was pietism. Lutheran pietists came from revival movements in Norway, Sweden, and Germany. They stressed personal devotion and fervor in faith. In morals, they rejected the kind of beer-drinking heartiness which the Americanizing Lutherans and Old Lutherans alike enjoyed.

Through the years almost all these Lutherans except the Missouri and Wisconsin synods have overcome old rivalries and moved toward union. Most Lutherans do not want to stand apart as the only "pure" church. In the 1980s Lutherans moved toward a merger designed to include two out of three people of their faith in America. The majority has shown that it can be faithful to its heritage and still cooperate with other Christians, not least of all Catholics.

Despite their profound loyalty to the American cause, Lutherans of German descent suffered much when America fought Germany during World War I. After that war, more of them dropped the use of the German language from their worship and schools. In many other ways Lutherans in the twentieth century showed that they were at last "at home" in the American climate. Lutherans found they never had to give up their gospel of forgiveness of sins to be Americans.

●

28 Dutch Reformed Christians

John Calvin, 1509-1564
Early Reformed Leader

Dutch Reformed churches are divided into two denominations: Reformed Church in America, and Christian Reformed Church. Like the Lutherans, they had differences about how Americanized they should be.

In that part of Typical City where the Lutherans are likely to be, the visitor will also find a Dutch Reformed congregation. The denominational name might be either Reformed Church in America or the Christian Reformed Church. Churches in these groups are most common in New York, New Jersey, Michigan, and Iowa, for these are the Dutch strongholds.

It may seem confusing to talk about Reformed churches, since one would think that all churches of the Reformation—Anglican, Lutheran, Baptist, and the like—should be called that. But people have come to use that

Norman Vincent Peale, above, and Robert Schuller, below, prominent ministers of the Reformed Church in America

name only in connection with the churches influenced chiefly by the reforms of John Calvin, most of which were from Switzerland, France, the Netherlands, and certain parts of Germany. In America most churches called Reformed were either Dutch or German.

Depending upon which of the two denominations one stumbles upon, there will be somewhat different emphases. The first, the Reformed Church in America, tracing roots back to colonial times, is more adapted to the American setting. Some of the best-known congregations in America are of this group. Millions, for example, have known of New York's

Marble Collegiate Church or California's Crystal Cathedral because of the prominence of their ministers, Norman Vincent Peale and Robert Schuller. Both of them used their pulpits and other media—radio, television, or publishing—to spread messages of "positive thinking" or "possibility thinking." They may not be typical of the Reformed churches because John Calvin—who stands behind the Reformed tradition—had gloomier views of human potential than Peale and Schuller. Yet both men insist that they are at home on the soil prepared by their Dutch forebears.

The second group, the Christian Reformed Church, shares Michigan and Iowa with their kin church, but is less well represented in the East. In the middle of the nineteenth century new immigrants believed they would be freer off by themselves in the woods and villages of the Midwest. To keep the purity of their doctrine and remain loyal to their old ways, they kept their distance from their more Americanized cousins in the Reformed Church in America and were suspicious of other Protestants.

While the Netherlands was long a commercial power, its government did not encourage emigration, so in colonial times the Dutch founders of New Netherlands were not numerous. In 1857 the Dutch churches split into two groups. The Christian Reformed Church received many of the new Midwestern immigrants, but the Reformed Church in America kept most of the congregations in the East, concentrated in New York and New Jersey. Both denominations set up colleges and seminaries in Michigan.

Many Dutch immigrants were poor, so they wanted both economic opportunity and religious freedom when they came to America under several leaders, including the Reverend Albertus C. Van Raalte (1811-1876). In 1846 Van Raalte and 100 others arrived in New York, but they were soon in conflict with the Dutch leadership there. They eventually arrived in Michigan, a state that was eager to attract a new immigrant population. The minister stayed, naming his colony there "Holland." Soon a cluster of villages developed as these poor and hardy Netherlanders hacked out a miniature of the Dutch countryside and town life in the demanding Michigan climate. The Dutch settlements became the center of furniture-making in America.

Under the leadership of Reformed pastor Albertus Van Raalte, Dutch immigrants settled in Holland, Michigan.

Throughout the century, Dutch pastors brought whole congregations over from Holland and, with them, chose the denomination with which to affiliate. Those who chose Van Raalte's group were eager to keep Dutch customs and practices.

But Van Raalte eventually came to be on the more moderate side, that of the Reformed Church in America. The more conservative group, the Christian Reformed Church, founded parochial schools to nurture the children apart from the American public school environment where they thought their faith might be compromised.

The visitor to a Reformed Church which is conscious of its heritage will find the congregation expecting to hear strong sermons on biblical themes. During services while the minister expounds the scripture, the congregation participates in solemn prayer and plain styles of hymnody. The church itself is likely to be simple in design. Though possessing an eye for beauty, Dutch Reformed Christians abhorred the idea of including many statues or pictures in the church. The proportion, simplicity, and "holy emptiness" of such Reformed churches is impressive.

The Reformed Church in America is in the Protestant mainline. On the other hand, the Christian Reformed Church is more reluctant to enter this scene, and is known for the warmth of its own congregational life.

The inscription in the German language on the cornerstone of this church shows its origin as a German Reformed congregation. Today most German Reformed churches are part of the United Church of Christ.

ST. PAUL UNITED CHURCH OF CHRIST

ZUR EHRE GOTTES
SANKT PAULUS
REFORMIERTE
GEMEINDE
JUNI 1826

29 The United Church of Christ: The German Reformed Heritage

The German Reformed tradition in 1957 helped create a new church body: the United Church of Christ. Among notable American churchmen from this tradition are historian Philip Schaff and theologians Reinhold and H. Richard Niebuhr.

Not far down the street from the Lutheran building in our Typical City is a German Reformed church. Present members, however, have not clung to a separate identity. The visitor will not find the name "German Reformed" or "Evangelical and Reformed" on the church sign of any buildings in America today—unless in small print under the name United Church of Christ. Perhaps in older buildings there is either a German or English reference to "Reformierte" or "Reformed" church life chipped into the concrete.

It may seem curious to visit a group of Protestants whose church body no longer exists independently, yet it makes sense to do so because the Reformed church tradition lives on. Mergers of the sort that blended Congregationalists with the Evangelical and Reformed Church in 1957 do not snuff out centuries' worth of churchly custom, belief, or habit. So a stop at a congregation which used to be German Reformed remains worthwhile.

A United Church of Christ, alias Evangelical and Reformed, alias German Reformed, congregation, in its worship will seem to the casual observer like a blend of Lutheranism and Congregationalism. The preacher will expound the Bible. Yet the merger has helped the Reformed Church discover the Congregational heritage, a tradition that has been longer at home in English-speaking America. Whoever stays after church to hear the congregation discuss its place in the world will likely find members more ready to take stands on public and political issues than are most Lutherans.

The German Reformed began to come in numbers in the middle of the nineteenth century. When the very first such German Protestants began to trickle into Pennsylvania a century earlier, Benjamin Franklin was worried: What would these "Palatine [German] boors" do to the old population? Might they not Germanize the others before the others turned them into English types? Yet poor and suffering Germans kept arriving in Pennsylvania and New York. When America was founded, there were 201 Reformed congregations of German background. This number led them to be ranked sixth largest in the colonies. In 1957, after a merger in 1934 with midwestern Evangelicals who were also of German stock, there were 810,000 members in 2,740 churches.

When many Germans settled in Pennsylvania in the mid-1700s, Benjamin Franklin worried about their influence on the English-speaking colonists.

These Americans of German stock contributed greatly to American religious thought: Reinhold Niebuhr, top, Richard Niebuhr, middle, and Philip Schaff, bottom.

This rather small church body left large marks on American religious thought. Two midwestern Evangelicals of German stock, brothers Reinhold Niebuhr (1892-1972) and H. Richard Niebuhr (1894-1961), taught at New York's Union Seminary and at Yale Divinity School. They are certainly the two most influential native-born American theologians of the twentieth century. But the German Reformed also contributed greatly to religious thought in the nineteenth century. They had a tiny seminary in the backwoods at Mercersburg, Pennsylvania, that wrote large chapters in church history. One of its leaders, John Williamson Nevin, worked for Christian unity using "high church" models of tradition that made him sound almost Anglican. He stressed frequent celebration of the Lord's Supper.

Better known for his Reformed vision was Nevin's Mercersburg colleague Philip Schaff (1819-1893). Schaff, like many other people in this Reformed heritage, came from German-speaking Switzerland. He admired the American churches of English descent because they were so full of activity, so ready to grow, so rich in optimism. But he thought they were too divided. He admired the scholarship and deep thinking of European churches like his own. He wanted to combine the best features of English-speaking and German church traditions.

Schaff, who later (1870-93) taught at Union Seminary in New York, wrote a book called *America* to explain his new environment to Europeans. He also produced a six-volume history of the Christian Church to help give Americans a deeper sense of their religious past. His mild friendliness to some Catholic ways led his enemies to accuse him of "popery," but Schaff survived their charges. Near his death, when people of all faiths gathered for a World Parliament of Religion during the Chicago World's Columbian Exposition of 1893, Schaff bestirred himself one last time to promote Christian unity.

His fellow German Reformed Christians, standing in his tradition, took the great step in 1957 of uniting with Congregationalists. In this merger, churchgoing Americans for the first time leaped the bounds of their ethnic groups and truly blended their traditions. The "Palatine boors" were Americanized, and the heirs of Schaff proved they had gotten the message. ●

30 Eastern Orthodox Christians

Most Christians from eastern Europe belong to the Orthodox Church. Orthodox worship is rich in light, color, incense, and ceremony. Today many Orthodox live under Communist governments.

Icons (religious paintings, usually on wood) and richly ornamented crosses are among the articles used in Orthodox worship. The distinctive style and design of these articles originated hundreds of years ago.

Eastern European Christians and Jews came a half century later than did the great waves of immigrants from western continental Europe. They were Orthodox Christians, often Russian or Greek but quite possibly Croatian, Albanian, Serbian, or a score of others. They came in the early 1900s, usually because of the lure of prosperity in the New World. Only 26 out of 1,000 American church members are Orthodox, which does not give Americans a fair picture of the role of Orthodoxy in the whole Christian world, where it numbers at least 76 million people.

The visitor to an Eastern Orthodox service of worship will be dazzled by the splendor of light, color, incense, sound, and movement. Ordinarily the worshipers stand as the priests enact the Eucharist, the rites of the Divine Liturgy, behind an "iconostasis" or barrier covered with holy pictures. Like Roman Catholics and high church Protestants, Orthodox Christians make much of the Eucharist. In some cases Orthodoxy's high holidays do not quite match those of the Western Church. Orthodox Easter, for instance, comes a bit later. The visitor may not understand all that goes on as the splendidly robed and usually bearded men hold services in Greek or Russian or some other language. They might find the services long and boring. Still, visitors cannot fail to be impressed by the sense of continuity and faithfulness.

Orthodoxy is distinctive among American Christian groups because it first came from the West Coast and not the East. The earliest Orthodox on American soil were Russians sent in the 1800s to engage in missionary work or to minister to Russian colonists in Alaska. Some of them made their way to Seattle and other northwest cities. Only later, around 1900, did hundreds of thousands of eastern Europeans, hence Orthodox Christians, arrive in the mining country of Pennsylvania and the industrial regions of eastern states.

Orthodoxy is distinguished by ethnic or national backgrounds, rather than by denominations. It is better to describe the general tradition than one individual's vision for it. Orthodoxy is the faith of the eastern half of the European Christian Church. For centuries it lived chiefly under Islamic domain; in this century it lives chiefly under Communism. This meant that Orthodoxy has had to develop an ability to get along with the powers that be, for

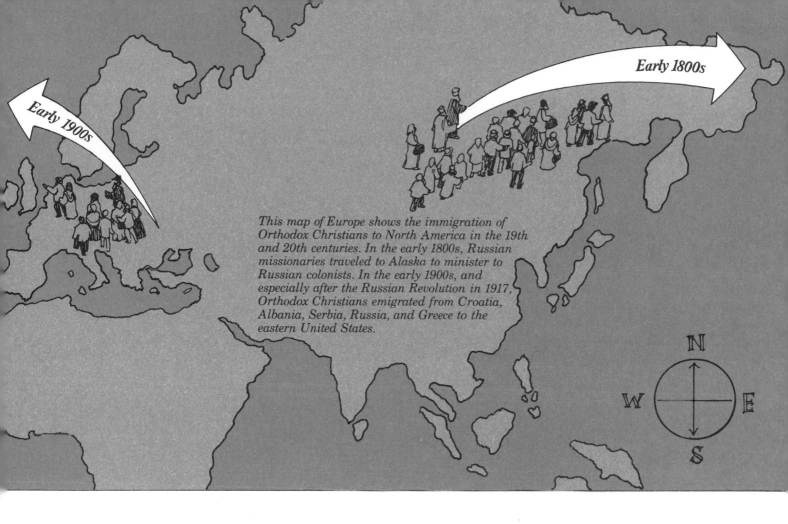

This map of Europe shows the immigration of Orthodox Christians to North America in the 19th and 20th centuries. In the early 1800s, Russian missionaries traveled to Alaska to minister to Russian colonists. In the early 1900s, and especially after the Russian Revolution in 1917, Orthodox Christians emigrated from Croatia, Albania, Serbia, Russia, and Greece to the eastern United States.

Early 1900s

Early 1800s

some centuries the tsars, and to specialize in what the church can do for the inner life, for a person's spirituality.

In 1054 European Christianity split into Roman Catholicism in the West and Orthodoxy in the East. Since then, Orthodoxy has seemed remote to Protestants and Catholics. In the twentieth century, however, the Christian unity movement finds Orthodoxy with Protestants in World and National Councils of Churches, and yet congenial to the Roman Catholic Church. Orthodoxy shares much with Catholicism but does not accept the authority of the pope.

It is the variety of national experiences that most nags and explains Orthodoxy. Who is legitimate, for instance: the Serbs who are related to churches that coexist with the Communist regime in Yugoslavia, or the Serbs who stand with their exiled monarchs and consider themselves to be loyal to a kind of church-in-exile alongside a government-in-exile?

The mixture of church names is colorful and confusing. There is an American Holy Orthodox Catholic Apostolic Eastern Church with 9,000 members and there are Albanian, Bul-

garian, and Romanian churches or episcopates. Almost 2 million belong to the Greek Archdiocese of North and South America. In 1922 these Greeks separated themselves from the church in Greece to organize themselves. They have been well led under notables like Archbishop Athenagoras and later Archbishop Yakovos.

As a result of the Bolshevik Revolution in 1917 and the persecution of much of the church in Russia, the Russian Orthodox Church in America has endured change and divisions. Meanwhile, more than 800,000 exiles have come since the Bolshevik Revolution including about 55,000 persons displaced after World War II. The storms of change swirl around Orthodoxy in the Islamic and Communist world. Yet hundreds of thousands of Orthodox find spiritual refuge in ethnic communities and the often lavish buildings they use to glorify God and to remember what they name and revere as Holy Tradition. They have not yet become familiar to the non-Orthodox majority in most communities and in the nation at large. ●

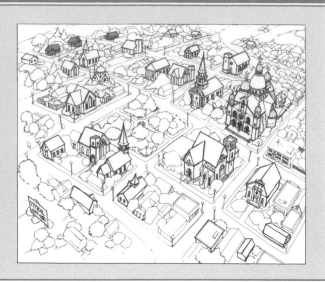

31 The Church of the Brethren

The Church of the Brethren, a small church with influence beyond its size, has roots in Germany. Its members faithfully opposed slavery and have been pacifists. While keeping their own identity, Brethren have worked closely with other churches.

In the country west of Typical City, people with sharp eyes are likely to spot several modest white or brick churches. They represent distinct minorities in American religion, yet each, at least in their earlier histories, has made a witness for peace and an impact far beyond their number of members. While several tiny groups of this sort exist, three stand out: the Church of the Brethren, the various Mennonites, and the Moravians. None of them is large. None is chiefly urban, though there are congregations in cities. They are not growing. Yet they have endured through the centuries and have found distinct missions.

The Church of the Brethren stands in a tradition that goes back to Reformation times, even if not formally organized in Germany until 1708. When the first settlers from this group came to Pennsylvania in 1719 they were called Dunkers. This pet name came from their well-known practice of dunking or immersing those who were being baptized.

The visitor to a Brethren congregation will find a warm circle of people who know each other well. Some of their practices help them stand out among denominations. For example, they have encouraged the keeping of the *agape* or love feast, after the practice of early Christians who shared a fellowship meal in addition to the Lord's Supper. At such love feasts the Brethren might engage in a foot-washing ceremony, following the example and command of Jesus. The observer may spot some bearded, suspender-wearing young men and some simply dressed young women. These have copied the clothes of their great-grandparents, finding in them models of the simple living that is part of the Brethren way.

There are only about 170,000 in 1,000 congregations, almost none of which are in the South or in great urban areas. The Brethren have not had any extremely well-known leaders since colonial times. From Pennsylvania villages their movement spread west under a succession of faithful lay and clerical leaders, none of whom stood out.

This leaves us free to pick a typical rather than an outstanding leader, a convert who grasped the Brethren vision. Henry Kurtz, a Lutheran minister in Pittsburgh, resigned his post and studied the forming of Christian community. He dreamed of building a colony called Concordia, but it never got off the ground. In 1828, at age 30, Kurtz was baptized as a Dunker in Ohio. Using his superior education, he soon rallied and led others of his outlook through the 1830s and 1840s. Finding that the public did not understand the ways of the Brethren, he thought it advisable to begin a church paper, which became the "Gospel Visitor." The paper printed letters and news from scattered Brethren.

These Brethren needed each other to build up morale. They did not always have an easy life in America. Their ancestors arrived just in time to bring their pacifist witness to bear against taking up arms in the Revolutionary War—a very unpopular stand. Then, before the Civil War, they took strong positions against slavery, thus making themselves controversial in southern states. But when war came, they again refused to bear arms, thus alienating northern warmakers. The peace churches never have had it easy in wartime, even if they have worked to bind up wounds, care for sufferers, and show loyalty to their country in other ways.

Through the years the Brethren won the respect of those who did not agree with them. Not content to restrict their outreach to peacemaking, they have also worked hard on relief overseas. For example, through Heifer Project International, an agricultural development organization, the farm-based denomination and other Christians help spread American agricultural wealth overseas. Not many Americans are choosing to become Brethren. Yet more have chosen to admire these spiritual cousins who have managed to keep a strong identity without really standing apart. The Brethren cooperate with the World and National Councils of Churches and in other ways show that, while they may be "out in the country," they are very much *of* the country, the nation, and the world Church. ●

"The Gospel Visitor," above, was founded by Henry Kurtz, a leader in the Church of the Brethren.

The foot-washing ceremony among the Brethren is a practice that follows the command and example of Jesus.

32 The Mennonites

The Mennonites, another "peace church" of European origin, have been persecuted by both Christians and non-Christians. They set an example of nonviolence and service. The Amish, the strictest Mennonites, try to do without modern conveniences such as cars and electricity.

Menno Simons, 1496-1561
Founder of the Mennonites

A little further out in the country beyond the Church of the Brethren is another "peace" church of continental European descent, the Mennonites. Like so many other churches which allow for great individual liberty, this one has seen many individuals taking the liberty of dividing the movement. Mennonites in America have developed a number of little denominations. The largest, called simply the Mennonite Church, has 100,000 members in over 1,100 churches, most of them in Pennsylvania or in states west from there to Kansas. There are Mennonite colleges in Virginia, Kansas, Indiana, and elsewhere.

Mennonite worship has much in common with Brethren styles. There are foot-washing, "believers' baptism" of adults, the celebration of "the kiss of peace" following the New Testament example—but with men and women separated for this ceremony. Worship is simple, and the sermon is likely to be unadorned, uncluttered with fancy rhetoric, and aimed at promoting the simple Christian virtues. The buildings will also be unadorned, with no statues or pictures.

The Mennonite tradition has been one of martyrs and long persecution. The movement was founded in Switzerland by people who thought that the radical reformer Ulrich Zwingli (1484-1531) had not gone far enough in reform. Particularly, Zwingli worked for a union of church and state. The followers of Menno Simons (1496-1561), a native of Holland, wanted that union broken. They were ready to suffer for their opposition, and they did.

Protestants and Catholics alike resented and harassed these simple people. Like many who are persecuted, they spread their movement wherever they fled. For example, many were chased from Germany into Russia from which, after both World Wars, many migrated to western Canada and the United States.

With the loss of German, Dutch, or Russian languages in America, many Mennonites have dropped their simple garb and ways and become much like other Protestants. However, the

Young Mennonites both at home and in distant places in the world give medical aid, provide agricultural help, and serve in many other ways.

exile movement from Russia and elsewhere to America assures a constant renewing of the distinctive Mennonite way.

As early as 1643 a Jesuit found some "Menists" on Manhattan. Ever since, Mennonites have come in waves, usually as a result of squeezes put upon them in European wars and persecutions.

Mennonites had a hard time, as did the Brethren, for their willingness to be Christ's "victim" people. They suffered abuse and turned the cheek in the face of enemies. They were nonresistant people, unwilling to bear arms, though many of them did hospital work in the Revolutionary and Civil Wars. Like the Quakers they roused suspicion by being unwilling to take oaths. Along with many other withdrawn groups, they hold to high standards of church discipline.

The Amish are split off from the main movement in order to hold to the strictest standards. They entered American folklore as bonnet-wearing, black-clad women, blue- and black-overalled or suspendered boys, clear-skinned girls, people who drive buggies and want to do without cars, electricity, and many modern conveniences. Within their group they are fun-loving and warm. They have been very productive farmers, sometimes resented because they use their prosperity to buy more land, rather than to plow money back into the merchant economy of the nearby towns. Amish have won the right not to send their children to public high schools, where they might be tainted by practices of the general population. They usually run their own grade schools. They tend to be admired for the clarity and courage of their convictions, but not followed, because the demands of their tradition do not seem workable in complex, urban America.

The Mennonite Church, on the other hand, tries to blend the old discipleship with new participation in the world. Mennonites have been among the pioneer conscientious objectors in American society, pacifists who, instead of retreating to the hills, have entered the mainstream of society to carry out their vision of discipleship. Their influence has spread to people who do not share their rather strict observances.

Mennonites send young people around the world, not so much to convert the heathen as to be of service. They have built refugee camps, collected funds for the hungry, and sent agricultural experts overseas to help nations develop better crops. At home in America they also specialize in relief. After earthquakes or tornadoes their volunteers are often the first rebuilders on the spot. Many people around the world who never have heard of Menno Simons have profited from the efforts of his disciples. ●

33 The Moravians

The Moravian Church, the oldest Protestant church body, is known for its music and its worldwide missions. David Zeisberger was a famous Moravian missionary to the American Indians in the late 1700s.

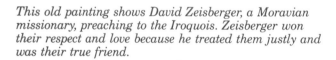
This old painting shows David Zeisberger, a Moravian missionary, preaching to the Iroquois. Zeisberger won their respect and love because he treated them justly and was their true friend.

A third small church with continental roots, peace-minded but today seldom ranked as a "peace church," is the Moravian. The visitor will more likely find a Moravian church in small towns or cities in Pennsylvania around Bethlehem, or in North Carolina around Winston-Salem, than elsewhere. Both these cities were colonial Moravian settlements. There is a string of Moravian churches across much of the upper two-thirds of America as far west as North Dakota. Wherever they are, Moravians feel a little like an extended family. Sometimes they even speak of one another using the rather quaint terms "brother" and "sister."

The Moravians are a singing fellowship. Anyone fortunate enough to find one of the 150 congregations and join in with the 55,000 members is in for a musical treat. A Moravian

Musical Foundation tries to recover music by Moravian composers, some of it lost in church attics since the early 1800s. Hymnsinging is often accompanied by "trombone choirs" or brass ensembles. At love feasts on Christmas Eve and other occasions the choir sings while the people in the pews drink coffee or cocoa and eat moderately sweet rolls. Then, gooey hands on hymnbooks, the congregation takes over with lusty song while the choir rests. Perhaps the trombone players eat and drink after the service?

A hundred years before Martin Luther, John Huss (1369-1415), a reformer from Bohemia, now part of Czechoslovakia, started a movement which these Bohemian and Moravian "Brethren" kept alive. For a century they led the fight against papal rule, had their own

Moravian Archives, Bethlehem, Pennsylvania

nia. Zinzendorf himself came a year later to give leadership.

David Zeisberger (1721-1808) was a Moravian of vision. Born in Europe, he worked among American Indians from 1745 to 1808, at a time when most other Protestants had lost taste for this mission. Zeisberger studied Iroquoian languages, and then in the Iroquoian longhouses he spread a message of peace and taught Moravian devotional styles. He persisted in this work, despite occasional outbreaks of hostilities between Native Americans and whites and with little encouragement from any except fellow Moravians.

Most other colonists simply took Indian lands when they wanted them. But the Indians exempted Zeisberger when they accused the white race of robbing and mistreating them: He was truly their brother. As Indians were removed further West, he went with them into Ohio, where he helped them build little communities. Even there, though he was a man of peace, Zeisberger was arrested in 1781 because the British thought he was working for the American revolutionaries.

While he was gone, American troops stupidly and cruelly massacred at least 100 of Zeisberger's friendly Indians, while a few survivors had to watch their modest villages burn. Their friend the missionary did not tire. Zeisberger followed the refugees further northwest into Michigan and Canada. In the end he was more identified with the Indians than with the Moravians.

Not all Moravians have Zeisberger's kind of courage or staying power, but their continuing missionary activities on several continents have made them a worldwide church in which only one member in five has a white skin.

Zinzendorf, the eighteenth-century patron of the Moravians, wanted to work for Christian unity and did not even think of the Moravians as another denomination. He considered them an "ecclesiola," a "little church" of devout mission supporters in established churches. As so often happens, this man of cooperative spirit was rejected by Christians of other churches for promoting what they regarded as a sect of his own.

The Moravians, small as they are, are not an eccentric sect but a group of hospitable and generous Christians. ●

"Protestant" interpretation of the Lord's Supper, stressed Bible reading, and took the path of non-resistance. Although there aren't many records from the early years, Moravians place their formal start in the year 1457.

For all of this they suffered. When Europe turned half Protestant and fought religious wars, they had to flee or go underground. In the 1720s, some found their way to the estate of a devout German Lutheran, Count Ludwig von Zinzendorf (1700-1760). Instead of converting them, he was himself converted. Soon Zinzendorf and these Moravians were devoting all their energies to spreading the gospel to persons in every corner of the world, including the American Indians. Some Moravians came to Georgia on a ship with John Wesley, but the more permanent settlers arrived in 1740 in Pennsylva-

Turn-of-the-Century Movements

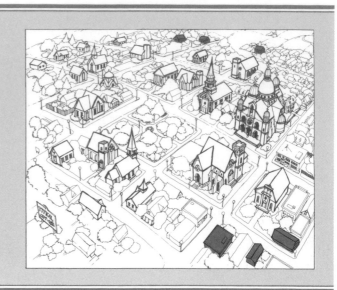

34 The Seventh-day Adventists

Seventh-day Adventists worship on Saturday (the seventh day) instead of on Sunday and stress the Second Coming of Jesus Christ. Good health and medical care are a third emphasis of this made-in-America church.

The Seventh-day Adventists take literally the Old Testament commands to keep the Sabbath on Saturday. To them, the move from Sabbath to Sunday observance was made under the ancient church of Rome. This opinion won Adventism an undeserved reputation for being anti-Catholic in their personal relations with Catholics.

The Adventist church building will probably be new; the movement is growing fast. The Adventists' house of worship will probably be in the part of Typical City where we find Southern Baptist and other fast-growing conservative Protestant churches.

Sabbath worship is one distinctive characteristic of Adventism, but there are at least two others. The name Adventism comes from the church's preoccupation with the return of Christ. Adventists believe that only when Jesus comes again, after some bad times, will good things happen. Before that time Christians should put their energies into expressing their faith and being personally good, but not necessarily setting out to change the world.

Adventism was a very common interest, almost an obsession, in America in the 1840s. Among the many Bible students who took the prophesies of the end seriously and then set dates predicting it was William Miller (1782-1849). He picked a day in 1843, and then again in 1844, for the Second Coming. Setting the date was his mistake. Many followers were disappointed when it did not come. Many outsiders made fun of the Millerites. Miller kept reinterpreting the reason for a delayed Second Advent. There may have been 50,000 Adventists when he was in his prime. Many stayed even after what they called the Great Disappointment. The movement split up; some groups, like the Advent Christian Church, survive today.

The prevailing denomination, Seventh-day Adventism, got its new start under the impulse of Ellen Gould White (1827-1915). She is less well known than Mary Baker Eddy, but her movement has been even more successful than Eddy's Christian Science.

White added the third part to the Adventist package: good health. Injured by a rock thrown by a playmate, young Ellen Gould Harmon was disfigured and often ill. After she was converted and became interested in religion, she turned Millerite. Meanwhile she claimed over 2,000 visions. She gained some influence when she married Adventist preacher James S. White, but she soon outshadowed him.

Members have studied White's recorded visions with care. She did not claim that they were on a par with the revelation in the Bible, but many followers regard them to be something like inspired scriptures. Increasingly, White's writings disclosed her concerns about health. Teamed with several members of the Kellogg family of Battle Creek, Michigan, Mrs. White's followers developed sanitaria, hospitals for long-term patients. She advised health procedures like vegetarianism.

E. G. White Estate

Ellen Gould White, 1827-1915
Founder of the Seventh-Day Adventists

In 1855 the Adventists planted their headquarters in Battle Creek, Michigan, which became a sanitarium and cereal-manufacturing center. In 1860 the denomination took the name Seventh-day Adventists. White used her energies to oppose the eating of meat, the drinking of alcohol, smoking, or engaging in too frequent sexual activities. White lived on until 1915, by which time Adventism was strongly established.

Today the Seventh-day Adventist Church is one of the fastest growing groups in America. Almost 600,000 U.S. members congregate on Saturdays in nearly 4,000 centers. They have made medical care a specialty, and sponsor a medical school in California and hospitals around the world.

For all their belief in the imminent end of the world, the Adventists seem optimistic, buoyant, concerned for their own and others' well-being. Because they wanted to protect their rights to worship on Saturday without being penalized by Sunday-closing laws, they became especially sensitive to the issue of religious freedom. Their magazine *Liberty* pleads the rights not only of Adventists but also of other vigorously dissenting minorities. ●

35 The Church of Christ, Scientist

The Church of Christ, Scientist, originated in 1876 in America. Its founder, Mary Baker Eddy, believed that suffering and illness are mental problems that can be cured by dispelling the sick person's illusions.

Mary Baker Eddy, 1821-1910
Founder of the Church of Christ, Scientist

Another "made in America" church body that has always inspired curiosity and awakened controversy is the Church of Christ, Scientist. Its members are usually called "Christian Scientists." The mother church, or headquarters, in Boston keeps the records and does not share them with the public. Therefore no one has statistics concerning membership. In the 1970s the church experienced considerable losses in membership; estimates are that about half a million Americans still have ties to the movement.

The Christian Science churches often look like Greek temples. They signal solidity, stability, security, and timelessness. The interiors are usually quite formal and sober, lacking much decoration. The sign in front of each church announces the topic for the week, for example, "Mind," or "Truth," or "Spirit." Each week every Christian Science group has the same topic. These messages are sent out from headquarters to be put to use by readers. Christian Science, which depends much on literacy, has established attractive and sedate reading rooms in many communities. There the highly-respected daily newspaper the *Christian Science Monitor,* founder Mary Baker Eddy's book *Science and Health with Key to the Scriptures,* and other church literature are available.

Mary Baker Eddy (1821-1910) belongs to that small rank of well-remembered founders in American religion. An heir of New England Congregationalism, the founder of Christian Science knew many misfortunes and suffered three not very happy marriages. For a time she lived a wandering existence among relatives and in boarding houses. But the upsets of those years all were being put to good purposes. She was gathering thoughts about science and health. After she fell on the ice and claimed to be cured of a broken hip through spiritual techniques, she attracted more attention to herself as a healer.

This First Church of Christ, Scientist, built in 1894 in Boston, is the "mother church" of this "made in America" denomination.

Mrs. Eddy came to develop a complex view of health. Some followers later wanted to revere and even come close to deifying her. She claimed only, however, that a new light was being shown into the world and that she simply had happened to be standing nearest the window. Yet she was self-assured about her views, which contradicted those of the Christians around her. God revealed himself to her as Eternal Mind, which is reflected in human life. She taught people to mistrust the world of the senses and to see suffering and death as mental problems, illusions. The Christian Science practitioners, as the healers are called, concentrate on helping people dispel illusions.

In 1876 Mrs. Eddy founded the Christian Science Association. By 1892 she had reorganized her institution into a tightly controlled body. So gifted an administrator was she that her movement survived a number of schisms.

Critics abounded. Mark Twain and other humorists used satire to diminish her reputation. Suspicious literary detectives claimed to find that she copied other persons' writings and was not always honest. Leaders of traditional Christian churches staged conferences to demolish her views and tried to sway audience sympathy away from her.

The Church of Christ, Scientist survived because it addressed the needs of people at the turn of the century. A century before Mrs. Eddy, a New England woman would ordinarily have had to be a victim of her own hard schedule. As life eased, women had more time to devote to comfort and self-improvement. Many of them described new diseases, or new names for old diseases. Mrs. Eddy told them that what was wrong with them was giving in to Matter, living with the illusions of pain and illness.

Christian Science never used aggressive means to recruit, but depended in a way on word-of-mouth endorsements. As more citizens pay attention to spiritual healing, Christian Science has met more intense competition from other religious groups. The church has survived hard times before. Most members keep their faith in the movement that they insist has helped them. ●

36 Jehovah's Witnesses

Jehovah's Witnesses, started in America in the late 1800s, reject other churches as being under the devil's power. Witnesses have many specific beliefs about the Second Coming of Christ. Some of their convictions, such as refusing blood transfusions, lead to trouble with the government.

Among the new American faiths of the last century Seventh-day Adventism has moved quite close to conservative Protestantism on many issues, and Christian Science seems to be less a subject of controversy. But a third new group, called Jehovah's Witnesses, still awakens furies. The visitors seeking its church will find a sign reading "Kingdom Hall" on architecturally modest, undistinguished buildings. If it is a bit further down the block in Typical City than the other churches, this is because the Witnesses stand off by themselves. Theirs is the only large American church that openly rejects all others. They even see the ministry of other Christians as being somehow under the kingdom of Satan. Similarly, Jehovah's Witnesses, while they are normally very strict and law-abiding, give no loyalty as such to the nation. They believe that the United States, as an earthly kingdom, is also under the power of God's enemy.

Such views are guaranteed to make Jehovah's Witnesses unpopular. In fact, being persecuted is to them a sign of their loyalty to God. Their Kingdom Hall is likely to be in the part of town where the upper lower class lives, for Jehovah's Witnesses is very much a movement associated with certain social classes. Since the Witnesses keep their social life pretty much to themselves, friendships between Witnesses and non-Witnesses are rare. Witnesses are familiar figures, however, since each member is supposed to give a certain number of hours per week to the cause. They do this by selling the *Watchtower* magazine, distributing literature, or making intense efforts at converting others by house-to-house calling.

An outlook so different from that of other churches had to derive from a strong personal vision. The founder was Charles Taze Russell (1852-1916), president of his Watch Tower Bible and Tract Society from 1884 until the time of his death.

Though not well educated, Russell set up his own Bible study program, as have many other individualists in American history. He sold thousands, then millions of copies of his little books as he went around starting congregations. Russell permitted the use of several names for his followers, including Millennial Dawnists, International Bible Students, and even Russellites. He authorized a fresh translation of the Bible. In this version the name of God was translated "Jehovah," an old but inaccurate rendering, instead of the more common "Lord" or "Yahweh." Because of this, the movement came to be called Jehovah's Witnesses.

Russell argued that in 1914 Jesus had already come back to earth, but not in such a way that people could see him. According to Russell, Jesus was assigned to build a Kingdom on earth, technically a "theocracy," since God, not the people or earthly rulers, would have the power. Believers will witness the battle between God and his enemies but will not be called upon to fight in it. God will rule thereafter for 1,000 years, Russell said, and only 144,000 special believers will live in heaven. The wicked will simply be abolished from existence.

Charles Taze Russell, 1852-1916
Founder of Jehovah's Witnesses

Library of Congress

When World War I came, the movement got into trouble because it would take no part in siding with the United States against Germany. In fact, a federal court came as close as courts ever have come to acting against a religious faith in an effort to stamp it out. In due course, as passions cooled, the court reversed itself, and the Russellites or Jehovah's Witnesses prospered again, under the leadership of Judge Joseph F. Rutherford.

Again and again Jehovah's Witnesses have been in trouble with the law. They distributed tracts where it had been illegal to do so, and won rights to pass them out. They resisted blood transfusions on the basis of a special reading of a biblical passage. The courts occasionally intervene and order transfusions. Witnesses refused to salute the flag but were declared free from the practice on grounds of religious freedom. They are dissenters against governments everywhere from black Africa to the Soviet Union. Again and again they experience losses because of predictions about the end-time that do not become obviously true. Then they find a new set of people to convert—recently, for example, many American blacks—and recoup their losses.

Jehovah's Witnesses are distrusted by most other Christians, and understood by almost no one else. However, many Christians envy the loyalty and dedication of the members who go to Kingdom Halls to await the final battle. ●

37 The Salvation Army

The Salvation Army is well known for its social services among the poor, but it is also a church body. William and Catherine Booth, who started the Army in 1860 in England, found that military discipline attracted people, and they formed their church along military lines.

Salvation Army Archives and Research Center

William Booth (1829-1912), shown above, founded the Salvation Army in England. He encouraged women to preach, and his daughter Evangeline (1865-1950), below, led the Army in the United States.

Salvation Army Archives and Research Center

Most Americans do not know where to find a Salvation Army "church," but they are likely to be aware of the Army's existence. While other Christians gather in buildings where only fellow members see them, the Salvation Army leaders, called officers, are highly visible. In American cities before Christmas they ring their little bells, and, their blue uniforms or carol-playing trumpeters gaining notice, they ask shoppers to drop dollars in their red kettles. These monies, the public knows, go to places where often only the Army will go. They are to serve the poor and destitute in the cities. Television programs at Thanksgiving or Christmas show people being sheltered and given a warm and festive meal, after singing some hymns, in Salvation Army shelters or great halls loaned for the purpose. But the Army serves people year-round.

Some people attending Salvation Army worship for the first time may think that, the uniforms aside, they are in a conservative but exuberant Methodist setting. The great difference between Methodism and the Salvation Army concerns the sacraments. In the words of the Army's *Handbook,* baptism and the Lord's

The first and main purpose of the Salvation Army is to preach God's message and change lives. This purpose is combined with works of service to the needy and to victims of disaster.

Supper are "not necessary to salvation...we do not observe them." Founder William Booth had heard too much controversy in churches over the sacraments and did not want them to divide his movement. Generally the Army mood is casual, and the music often first-rate, since many Salvation Army band members hold advanced music degrees. Persons who attend love to sing and clap hands. Members give testimony to their faith and call for repentance. Their God is benevolent and wants all to be saved; here again, they are like Methodists. They also believe that the goal of Christian life on earth is perfection.

One other feature about Salvation Army life and worship: In theory and often in practice, women are equals to men. From the beginning, founder William Booth encouraged women to preach. Evangeline Booth (1865-1950), daughter of William and Catherine, was the real leader of the Army in America for three decades after 1904.

The vision for this military-seeming branch of Christianity came from William Booth and his family. The movement was born in England and remains strong in the British Isles. William Booth (1829-1912) was ordained a Methodist, but he and his wife Catherine, "the Mother of the Army," broke away from Methodism. Their special ministry was among the victims of industrial England, the neglected people of the slums. When William Booth found that in such settings people consider military discipline to be attractive, he devised uniforms and ranks and adapted military language. The declaration of faith is called "Articles of War," while local assemblies are called "corps." Members are designated as soldiers under officers. All this may seem strange coming from a group that has peaceful intentions.

The Army, born in England in the 1860s, arrived in America in 1880. A group named Volunteers of America split from the Army under the leadership of Booth's son, Ballington (1857-1940). Still, the Salvation Army prevailed and won converts. Over 5,000 officers today lead some nearly 400,000 members in 8,500 meeting places. Their places of worship are not as well known as their places of service—a compliment to any church body!

Each corps welcomes visitors and hopes to win them as repentant converts, ready to sign the Articles of War. But joining is rather a strenuous business, for it commits the people to discipleship and discipline. Members are expected not just to talk about doing good, but to get their hands dirty. Army soldiers often go about Christian work in poorer parts of town, where other Christians are not ready to go.

For all their bustle and activity, for all their good works, Booth and his followers insist that their first and main purpose is to save people "by the power of the Holy Spirit combined with the influence of human ingenuity and love." Other churches share the Salvation Army's concern for preaching to change lives. But not many others are on the scene with mobile canteens, relief units on battlefields, summer camps, settlement houses, and centers for alcoholic treatment. So General Booth's Army will probably always be better known for its work than his message. That may be ironical, but it has well served people who found friends in the outstretched arms of Army people.

38 The Pentecostal Churches

The Pentecostal churches began in the twentieth century and exist in many varieties. Pentecostals believe in the baptism of the Spirit, an onrush of grace apart from the baptism with water. Healing and speaking in tongues are other characteristics.

In an expanding lower-middle-class part of Typical City is likely to be a Pentecostal church. Its movement was born early in this century. Today many know the word Pentecostal (or charismatic) because Catholics, Episcopalians, and other mainline Christians have "received baptism in the Holy Spirit." In the words of David Wilkerson, an oldline Pentecostal, as he spoke of a major Pentecostal practice of speaking in unrecognized tongues, "tongues moved uptown."

However, Pentecostalism remains a dominant form of Christianity among the lower or lower middle class in black and white America, and among the poor in other parts of the world. The Church of God in Christ, a black Pentecostal body, claims over 2 million members in almost 5,000 American churches. It is by no means alone among Pentecostal churches. Many grow very rapidly.

"The House of God Which Is the Church of the Living God, the Pillar and Ground of Truth" and "Latter House of the Lord for All People and the Church of the Mountain, Apostolic Faith": The visitor may smile to see such words painted on crude signs in abandoned stores, where the poorer Pentecostals worship, but what goes on inside is a very serious and alert response to the Holy Spirit.

Largely white Pentecostalism also goes under many names: Church of God of Cleveland, Tennessee, is a large body; there are "Door of Faith Churches of Hawaii" and there is a "Full Gospel Church Association, Inc." and even a small group known as the "Neverdies." The Pentecostal Holiness Church is much larger, nearer the mainline. The Assemblies of God, the largest group, with 1.8 million members is a well-established and fast-growing example.

These Pentecostals differ widely from each other, but they agree that somehow a second blessing, a "baptism in the Spirit," is an experience all Christians should have. It is an onrush of God's grace apart from the blessing that comes in the Christian sacrament of baptism. In its spirit people feel close to God; most of them then acquire the gift of speaking in tongues and interpreting tongues. Healing is also a major belief and practice.

The Azusa Street church in Los Angeles, where the Pentecostal movement began in 1906

Assemblies of God Archives

Talking and singing in tongues was a sign of the spiritual awakening among Christians on Azusa Street under the leadership of William Seymour.

Pentecostalism is largely a twentieth-century movement. Scores of evangelists had the Pentecostal vision in the same decades, but William Seymour is a good man to study. The movement was born integrated, though most churches later separated along racial lines. Seymour was a black. Born in Louisiana, no one knows when, in 1905 he started studying under Charles F. Parham. At a New Year's Eve service in Topeka, Kansas, in 1900, some of Parham's Bible students had experienced "speaking in tongues." This is a "gift of the Spirit" mentioned in the biblical book of Acts and in the writings of Paul.

In 1906, on Azusa Street in an old run-down neighborhood of Los Angeles, Seymour experienced speaking in tongues as a "third baptism." This was added to the original water baptism and the second, or spiritual onrushing sort. So began a three-year-long revival meeting. The people listening to Seymour spoke and sang in tongues—unrepressed speech in syllables that do not belong to any known language, but which other Pentecostals believe they can interpret. People sang and danced, waved their arms in the air, and were as free with bodily gesture as with song and shout and tongues. Most modern Pentecostals think of those Azusa Street gatherings as the beginning of their church movement, just as the first Christian Pentecost, recorded in Acts 2, is often thought of as the beginning of the Christian Church.

Newspaper reporters seemed to enjoy writing about the thousands of blacks and whites who crowded Seymour's Los Angeles assemblies. Had Seymour been a polished promoter, there would be suspicion about his views. But Pentecostals see in his experience true spontaneity, the working of the Holy Spirit, who is as free as the wind.

Many Pentecostals, mostly in the Southeast, found their way into denominations. Often they fought each other or split. The story of the growth of Pentecostalism would be complicated to tell. It is enough to say that today's many more prosperous types of Pentecostalism come from those humble roots. Every year thousands more join one of the many Pentecostal church bodies. Some Pentecostal evangelists or pastors have risen to the top in the field of televised religion. Gone, in large measure, are the rude and crude ways, the backcountry styles. The mainline churches have discovered

that many members have taken up speaking in tongues and some have joined Pentecostal churches. At the same time, the Pentecostals have moved toward the mainstream. If they move too far and leave their roots behind, something seen as a new movement of the Holy Spirit will likely fill the void and seek out the poor who find in Pentecostalism a bearer of hope and meaning. ●

Today, the message of Pentecostal churches is often spread through television. Some mainline churches, too, have taken up speaking in tongues.

39 The Fundamentalists

Fundamentalist church bodies were formed around the 1920s by Protestants who believed that their churches were adapting too much to modern ways and thought. There are also fundamentalists within mainline churches. Fundamentalists insist that the Bible is without error and have a strong sense of its authority.

John Gresham Machen, 1881-1937
Fundamentalist Presbyterian Scholar

In modern America, most people know the name fundamentalism. They think of it as a conservative and sometimes belligerent form of Protestantism. Strict in doctrine and morals, its members criticize all those who do not believe the Bible the way they do. They may not even pray with persons in other fundamentalist denominations if they do not agree on all details. Yet they make contributions to church life through the loyalties they inspire. And in the later part of the twentieth century they increasingly have become a political force, working to get their moral ideas to be a part of the law of the land. Among their concerns are pornography, abortion, homosexuality, and lack of prayer in public schools.

Fundamentalists work through television, direct mail, publishing, and great rallies. But where are their churches, since few say "Fundamentalist" on the door? Many fundamentalists are members of Southern or other Baptist churches. Several small Presbyterian bodies are fundamentalist split-offs. Many fundamentalists, who are very independent Christians, have organized into separate "Nondenominational" or "Undenominational" congregations. And others have linked together to form fundamentalist denominations. One catalog of fundamentalist bodies lists many which are unfamiliar to most Americans: Bible Fellowship Church, Fundamental Evangelistic Association, Incorporated, or Independent Fundamental Bible Churches. Most of these are very small.

Are the people in a fundamentalist church all militants who will pounce on heretics? Not ordinarily. They tend to be lower middle-class or upper lower-class people, so their church is not in the most fashionable part of town. Although fundamentalism was born in the North and is really dispersed throughout the country, its churches are very frequently in the South or Southwest. The place of worship is probably a modest building.

Hymns are fervent; the preaching is a literal expounding of the Bible; the moral demands are strict, the fellowship a strong "we" against "they" sort. Always there is a strong sense of authority and security; fundamentalists allow little room for doubts.

Fundamentalism was born in reaction against Protestants who were conservatives but were ready to adapt to modern ways and thought. After they lost denominational struggles in the 1920s, fundamentalists organized their own groups. Fundamentalists insist that the Bible is without error. Most of them believe that the Second Coming of Christ and a millennium or thousand-year earthly reign of Christ are in the near future.

Who had the fundamentalist vision? Many opponents picture them as hill-country people, crude, with gravy drippings on their shirts. Some of the leadership, however, were well-educated, often at Princeton Seminary. The most noted of these was John Gresham Machen (1881-1937), a Johns Hopkins University scholar who taught at Princeton Theological Seminary (1906-29) after studies in Europe. He knew the history of doctrine well, and warred against modernism in Presbyterianism. He wrote a famed book on *The Virgin Birth of Christ* to defend that teaching which many others questioned. His scholarly works were sober and steady, but he also came to be a tough fighter against modernizers and allied with people who used some raw tactics.

Not at home in moderate Presbyterianism, he helped establish a new Westminster Theological Seminary in Philadelphia and a new foreign mission board. In 1934 the Presbyterian Church found Machen guilty of going against his ordination vows. He was expelled and helped found a new denomination in 1936. In 1938 this group split, as some thought Machen, who had died in 1937, too liberal. Machen always fought for the truth as he saw it, winning grudging respect from foes whom he often outargued or outmaneuvered.

The fundamentalists, as they continue to lose some members to the moderate conservative groups who call themselves evangelicals, remain firm in their faith against all odds. In a world that seeks authority and security, there are always new recruits to replace those that drift off into moderation.

Fundamentalists fear church adaptation to modern ways and thought. They are very loyal to their churches and to their understanding of Christianity.

XI
Outside the Christian Circle But Part of the Story

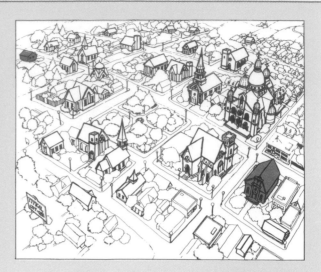

40 The Jews

Judaism in America has three major groups—Orthodox, Conservative, and Reform. Many American Jews today feel a twin obligation— to their heritage, symbolized by the nation of Israel; and to their country, America. The religious holidays are especially important in Jewish life.

To escape persecution in Europe in the late 1800s, thousands of Jews emigrated to America.

A visit to Christian denominations should have room for some detours. While this is not a history of all the religions in America—we cannot do justice to Scientology and Zen Buddhism and many others—one non-Christian form of worship is so interwoven with the churches that it merits an excursion. This is to the synagogue, the place of gathering for Jews.

If one counts the whole Jewish population in the census as a denomination, then 46 out of a thousand religious Americans are Jews, and Jews are the fifth largest religious bloc in the nation. Of course, these figures give a somewhat distorted picture. To be in the Jewish population, say Jews, is to be born of a Jewish mother, whether or not one practices the faith in the synagogue or believes in the God of Israel. The number of regular participants in Jewish *religious* life is a much, much smaller figure.

While the synagogue may be crowded with children attending Sabbath or Sunday Schools in communities where there are many Jewish children, the parking lot may not be so full of cars for adults on Friday evening or Saturday when Sabbath worship and gatherings are held. Only one Jew in five attends worship weekly, while in the nation as a whole, churched and unchurched alike, over 40% worship weekly.

Jews came to North American soil early; we know of some in New York in 1654. But there were only two or three thousand here at the birth of the nation, and there were no rabbis at all. By the middle of the nineteenth century, there were 77 Jewish congregations. Most of these were made up of Sephardic or southern European Jews. Later the Ashkenazic or northern Jews started to come, particularly from Germany. For a period of time, these Jews dominated.

The great immigrations of eastern European Jews in the late 1800s began after a purge or pogrom in the Pale of Europe—parts of today's Poland and Russia. They arrived victimized and penniless in New York and in other overcrowded cities. Many of them, uprooted from life in *shtetl* or village, dropped their loyalty to the synagogue.

Yet the synagogue survived. It became a rallying point after 1948 when Israel was formed, and when Israel was threatened in wars of 1967 and 1973. Jews also pondered the religious meaning of the Holocaust, Hitler's attempt to

Between 1933 and 1945, millions of Jews in Germany and other European countries suffered imprisonment and death.

exterminate them, and this sometimes led them back to synagogue.

Like Christianity, American Judaism is denominationalized. In Orthodox synagogues strenuous efforts are made to keep to Jewish practices in a Gentile world. Reform Judaism wants to adapt the faith to the American environment. Between them is an "historical school" called Conservatism, which is at home with modernity but also at ease with the tradition. There are extreme, small groups like Hasidism, an intense and almost mystically observant Judaism.

National Portrait Gallery, Smithsonian Institution, Washington, D.C.

Isaac Mayer Wise, 1819-1900
Influential Reform Jewish Rabbi

The shaper of Reform Judaism was Isaac Mayer Wise (1819-1900). It is worthwhile to focus on him because he was so eager to see Jews at home in America. Wise was educated in Europe. But he dreamed of America as his Zion and came in 1846 to be a rabbi in Albany and then in Cincinnati, a German Jewish center. Wise was as energetic as a Methodist circuit rider at rounding up Jews and getting them involved. He built a huge temple and held services that reminded many of liberal Protestant movements like Unitarianism. He headed Hebrew Union College from 1875-1900 and there influenced many rabbis.

One of the best-known incidents of his life occurred at a Hebrew Union College banquet. Shellfish was served, though it was a food forbidden to Jews. Wise had not taken care to have a kosher or "clean" kitchen. What was worse, when some Jews were offended over his departure from Jewish law, he made fun of them and took his critics lightly. This action of Wise was the last straw for some Jews. It confirmed their fears that he had abandoned their tradition. In response to Wise, these Jews became more conservative. Wise went his way, continuing to shrug off practices that he thought did not be-

This 1979 photo suggests the difficult environment in Israel, founded in 1948 to be a homeland for Jews, especially those who survived the Nazi persecution in Europe.

AP/World Wide Photos

"Why is this night unlike any other night?" This question is traditionally asked at the Passover Seder, the ceremonial family meal on the holy day when the Jews commemorate the deliverance of their ancestors from slavery in Egypt.

long in the modern world. Because, like most Reform rabbis, he repudiated Zionism—"America is our Zion," he said—Wise is less well-remembered today, but in his time he was as well-known as prominent Christian clergy.

Today Judaism struggles with the twin obligations to be faithful to its heritage, to the land of Israel, and faithful to the America in which its people have prospered. Jews have suffered anti-Semitism here, but never as much as in Europe. Jews are now very much at home in the America that once looked both attractive and forbidding.

There are times, however, when most temples are so crowded that you cannot get near them. Jews express their loyalties to the God of Israel and to Judaism chiefly at "high holidays." One of the major events is Rosh Hashanah, which means New Year, an autumn event after which there are Ten Days of Penitence. The prayers ask that the Lord will speed the day "when all men shall come to serve Thee."

The climax is Yom Kippur, the "Day of Atonement," the last of these Ten Days of Penitence. Non-Jews find worship on this occasion very doleful. For 24 hours people pray and fast, and members think through their faults. "Father, we have sinned against Thee." There are mournful chants and prayers as Jews try to refashion their spirits and lives. On Yom Kippur all observant Jews should be in the synagogue all daylight hours.

In spring comes Passover, in remembrance of the freedom of the ancient Hebrews from bondage in Egypt. This festival does not crowd synagogues because it is designed to be observed chiefly in homes with the Seder, a Passover meal. Minor festivals include *Sukkoth*, a kind of Thanksgiving Day for harvest, usually in October; *Hanukkah*, which celebrates ancient military victories, near the Christians' Christmas season; and *Purim*, a festive time recalling Jewish victory over Haman, a story told in the Book of Esther. ●

41 Native Americans

The Ghost Dance, a religious ritual of the western Plains Indians, is shown in this old painting. The United States government forbade the dance, believing that it encouraged Native Americans to resist U.S. national policy.

National Archives

**Native Americans had to fight for their identity as a people under the occupation and rule of white Americans.
They kept some of their traditional beliefs and forms of worship, and sometimes combined Indian lore with Christian themes.**

Visitors to a typical small city cannot find a church for Native Americans among the many ethnic parishes. Only in the biggest cities or near Indian reservations is there a largely Native American congregation. Most Indians do not live in the cities, fewer still are active Christians, and not many are organized into congregations.

The story of American Christianity is a story of tragic encounters between Indians and whites after the intrusion or invasion of Europeans. It is a tale with few happy pages. To find the Indian worshipers—whether they hold to their traditional Native American faith, whether they are conventionally orthodox Christians, or whether they blend the two religions—one must go to the reservations.

Most of the story of Protestant and Catholic Indian missions was over by the time the United States was born. Soon after 1776 the American government began the process of moving the remaining eastern Indians to western reservations.

After the Civil War, President U. S. Grant established a policy to have churches do much of the "civilizing," educating, and converting work. The natives had seen too much suffering to be easily converted by the whites who first displaced them and then took their lands. Life was demoralizing for Indian children, who in government schools were sometimes physically punished for speaking in their native languages.

Meanwhile, most Indians held on to their old ways. Fighting for their identity, they found what many people under attack have known:

114

Religion binds them to the past and unites them for the future. So Native Americans kept the traditional Sun Dance and Ghost Dance until the latter was forbidden by the U.S. government. The Ghost Dance was seen as a form of fanatical resistance to the national policies.

Who had the vision for Native American religion in the missionary era? Some missionaries, of course. But in fairness we should listen to a Native American, Black Elk. White poet John C. Neihardt studied Indian religion by gaining the confidence of Black Elk; Neihardt then wrote a book telling Black Elk's story. Neihardt wrote nothing about Black Elk's Christian side; in this chapter, however, we are interested in the special marks of traditional Native American religion.

Black Elk was born in 1863; his Oglala Sioux name was Ekhaka Sapa. As a thirteen-year-old he saw the Battle of the Little Big Horn, the Sioux stand against the United States army. He did not see the great Indian massacre at Wounded Knee, but he knew that there "in the bloody mud...a people's dream died."

Black Elk had many visions about his people, some of which foretold their sad future. Like so many Indians, he had a faith that united the tribes to nature and nature to the Great Spirit. His Indians loved the landscape and the wind and abhorred the violence which new settlers were doing to the open plains.

From a mountain top he prayed to "Grandfather, Great Spirit": "Again, and maybe the last time on this earth, I recall the great vision you sent me. It may be that some little root of the sacred tree still lives. Nourish it then, that it may leaf and bloom and fill with singing birds. Hear me, not for myself, but for my people; I am old. Hear me that they may once more go back into the sacred hoop and find the good red road, the shielding tree!... O make my people live!"

Yet the dispersal went on. What he called the sacred hoop, which bound Native Americans to nature and each other, was broken, and many people, along with their dreams, kept dying.

Many Native Americans have sustained something of their old religion and combined it with the missionaries' Christianity. Estimates run as high as 250,000 members in the Native American Church, best known for the legally permitted practice of chewing a hallucinogenic

Black Elk, 1863-1950
Oglala Sioux Leader and Seer

This photo taken in 1976 shows the first Native American in the Southwest to be ordained in the Catholic church administering Communion.

peyote button or seed, a mind-expanding drug. This church, organized in 1906, spent many years fighting for the legal use of the drug. Practices vary, but the church always looks to a shaman who controls the use of the peyote buttons. The words of the ritual combine some Christian themes with the Indian lore.

In this and other ways—far away from Typical City—the ancient settlers of North America continue to find meaning in an existence which has always threatened their survival and their ways of life. ●

115

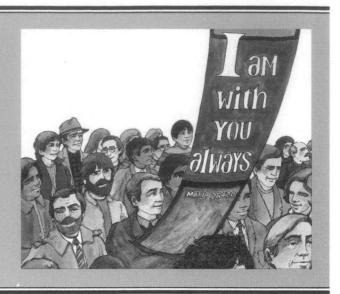

XII
Summing Up
American
Religion

42 Private Religion

Many people believe that they can be Christians without belonging to a church. This attitude is natural in a country with freedom of religion. But many Christians worry that people with this private religion will not pass the faith on to future generations.

When Americans tell the story of religion, they usually tell the story of churches, synagogues, temples, and other groups of people gathering to celebrate their faith. From the beginning, most religion has been a group activity. People in tribes gather for rituals to observe births, marriages, and deaths. They pray to produce or celebrate good weather or victory in war. The ancient people of God in Israel saw themselves being saved as a people, not just as individual persons. Paul called the Church the body of Christ, "one." Throughout Christian history the Church for most Christians has been a key part of their religion.

In the modern American world, the situation has changed. While the churches remain very strong, people have more and more thought of religion as an individual concern. They call it a "private affair."

In a free society religion becomes a matter of choice. Church members see the Church as a voluntary society, a gathering of like-minded people who agree on some purposes. If the Church is a voluntary form, it is not fully necessary. People consider themselves not only free to think for themselves, but also free to be Christian apart from church membership and churchgoing.

The idea of being individualistic or private about religion, a notion we take for granted today, had to get started somehow. In America we can trace certain definite steps. When the nation was born, some of the statesmen were of the Enlightenment. This movement called them to have faith in reason more than in revelation. The "Enlightened" believed that Jesus was a moral teacher, not the Son of God, and that the Church was dominated by priests who used "magic" to keep people loyal.

One of these Enlightened people was a British-born pamphleteer, Thomas Paine, who boosted the patriot cause. Churchgoers called Paine an atheist, an unbeliever. No, he said, he was not an atheist; but he had no need for a church. "My own mind is my temple." Another Enlightened person, President Thomas Jefferson, said that if he had to go to heaven with a group, he would not go at all.

Ordinary people tend to agree. Many of them are members of the Church. They welcome its place in society. At the same time, many others consider themselves to be "alumni" who no longer need it, once they have grown up. This is a problem for the loyal church members. They are concerned with more than the Church just surviving. But they also believe that if there is to be a Church in future generations they must convert and educate the young.

How do people remain religious without being part of the churches? Many do not. They drift away. Spiritual concerns simply die. Some get substitutes for religion in the clubs or movements to which they belong. Not a few read books to stimulate their religious ideas. Out of these they find or make up a faith satisfying to them.

In recent years, recognizing that some people are religious but not churchgoers, evangelists and religious entertainers have operated radio and especially television ministries. Most of them will tell people to go to the church of their choice. Yet by bringing church services into the home on Sunday morning and by ministering to people all week apart from the Church or the churches, some of these broadcasters are supporting "private religion" by implying that you can be a believer alone. You do not have to relate to anyone next to you in a pew. Some call this television ministry an "electronic church." ●

The idea that religion can be individualistic or private began in America's early days and was encouraged by a movement originating in Europe called the Enlightenment. Revolutionary patriots Thomas Paine, above, and Thomas Jefferson, below, were representatives of this movement.

Church leaders worry about "private religion." Such a concept means that people will not connect their faith with the world around them. You can make and remake private religion to suit your purposes. Many Christians doubt that private religion will ever transform a person with the power of the Word of God. Power to change the world through group action is missing. When two or three, or 2 million or 3 million, Christians band together, they can help feed the world, publish the Word, train ministers, and the like. Private religion cannot do this. "Do-it-yourself" spirituality of this private sort is hard to pass on to children. Although private religion allows for great freedom, it may be a bigger problem for church life than is unbelief itself. Yet, the existence of this "invisible religion" shows that people still hunger for God.

Some church leaders think that bringing religious services into the home via television encourages "private religion"—that is, religion that does not require belonging to a community of believers.

43 Civil Religion

Many Americans, both Christian and non-Christians, have a "civil religion," an unofficial faith with deep devotion to their nation and its symbols. Sometimes this faith can conflict with faith in God, but often it makes people better citizens and helps unite the nation.

Americans are not all unreligious, "privately" religious, or religious through church life. They have also found other ways to express faith, such as "civil religion," or "public religion."

Histories of the Christian Church usually concentrate on priests and ministers, missionaries and church buildings more than on what the people really believe or how men, women, and children behave. But people in churches also hold parallel faiths while they are Christian. For instance, some scholars observe one particular religion in America that exists alongside Christianity in the churches and helps unite the nation. This religion has no church buildings and no priests. Most people do not think of it as a kind of church. Yet observers who come from overseas notice it at once, and some historians think it is as important as church religion. This religion is the strong devotion and loyalty of Americans to the nation and a belief that the churches will help make people good citizens.

People from other countries notice that Americans' attitude of devotion and loyalty to their country is much like a religion. The respect for the Tomb of the Unknown Soldier in Arlington, Virginia, is one example of this "civil" or "public" religion.

AP/World Wide Photos

Another example is the fact that many Americans, like religious reformers, feel called by conscience to reform their country's laws. This attitude sometimes leads to demonstrations and protests, such as the one shown in the photo at left, and even to civil disobedience.

Benjamin Franklin called this faith "public religion." He was not interested in the churches' ways of saving souls, but he supported churches because they taught morality and helped support "public virtue" and the common good. Historian Sidney E. Mead called this faith "the religion of the republic." He thought it was a rival to Christianity, but a good-natured one that allowed the churches a place. Yet this faith of the republic was interested only in what churches did to promote the public moral patterns.

On the one hand, extreme critics say that civil religion is worship of the nation. Thus it is something that the churches should condemn. Modern nationalism can be an idolatry; it has taken ugly forms in some nations and been used to justify terrors. Nazism in Germany, Russian Communism, and Maoism in China are forms of nationalism that bear some of the marks of religion, while being godless. The nationalism of even more benevolent nations can look like religion. Americans are often more respectful of the holiness of the Tomb of the Unknown Soldier, a kind of national shrine, than they would be in a cathedral. They are more nervous about removing a national flag from their sanctuaries than they would be about removing the cross. They die for their country as they would not for their God.

On the other hand, other thinkers say that civil religion need *not* be idolatrous. It does not always compete with church religion. These thinkers remind us that the Bible *does* ask believers to support the rulers and the state. Believers can pray for leaders without worshiping the nation. Such prayers are not confined to just one church; people of many different denominations come together for such prayer. When there are many separate religious groups, people need some faith or some sacred symbols in common if they are to promote the morals and morale of the nation.

Civil religion has its shrines and its symbols, as well as creeds, saints, and prophets. Abraham Lincoln said that the Declaration of Independence was the creed, the statement of faith, of his "political religion." It is interesting to note that the Declaration was written by Jefferson, the Founding Father who had least use for the churches. And it was praised by Lincoln, the only president who was not a church member, however well he knew the Bible.

The Declaration's creed says that all persons are "endowed by their Creator" with unalienable rights, that all are created equal. This is part of the American faith. Many of the founders thought that all religions should teach that there is some sort of God, that people have to be moral, that they will be rewarded or punished. (This is not what many Christians think is central to their faith, but most Christians think that their faith also includes this understanding.)

Abraham Lincoln (1809-1865) is often seen as the greatest prophet of the American civil religion. He stands at the center of American history. Through the bloodshed of the Civil War the nation was "redeemed" from the sin of slavery and spared division and future internal warfare. Abraham Lincoln had a very strong faith in the Union and almost made it the center of his religion. Yet, say his admirers, he refrained from making an idol of the United States. He saw it as a nation "under God" and wanted all sides in politics and both sides in

Abraham Lincoln, shown above, is often seen as the greatest prophet of civil religion because of his great faith in the Union.

the Civil War not to claim that God was on their side. They should try to learn God's will and try to act in accord with their understanding of it.

Many presidential inaugural addresses talk about God and the nation. They sound like sermons in American civil religion. The national anthem is a kind of hymn. The flag is a symbol of that faith. People die for that faith. Most do not see it as a competitor to, but a parallel with, the Christian religion of their churches. American believers still for the most part want to "obey God rather than men," including public men. ●

What will happen to the churches in the years ahead? Believers and nonbelievers will continue to live side by side. But Christians have the promise that the Spirit of God and the love of Jesus Christ will be with them always.

The Christian churches have been in the Western hemisphere for almost 500 years, one fourth of the life of the whole Christian Church. They have been represented on the soil of the United States since early in the sixteenth century. When the nation was born, the churches were still small and weak. They held the loyalty of only a small percentage of the American people. Through the years they have grown. At almost any time between 1776 and the present, the graph lines on charts of church membership go higher and higher.

That upward moving line leveled off and began slowly to move downward in the 1960s and 1970s. This has led some people to ask about the future of the churches. The world in which the Christian Church has lived for twenty centuries has not been hospitable to its claims. The idea that the world was sinful and needed rescue by Jesus Christ's activity insults those who like to think that humans can make it on their own. The preaching that a particular story, the salvation story in the Bible, represents truth can make Christians sound very exclusive. We live in a nation and a world where Christian and non-Christian, believer and nonbeliever, must live together. The history of religious wars shows how bad the alternatives are. So some worry that Christian claims to truth will lead to conflict.

Throughout American history some church people have gone out hunting for "infidels," persons who they thought were faithless enemies of the Church. They have given such people, few as they are, great publicity. Militant believers can use the outsiders or the dissenters to frighten people: Beware, they say, because there are enemies of the faith out there. In recent times some have even spoken of a "secular humanist conspiracy."

The American climate is in many ways "secular," which means that people make up their minds about things the same way whether or not God exists. Some people do not believe in God, and they call themselves atheists. There is certainly much "humanism" of a godless sort, which contends that humans are the measure of all things. Many Americans want to be moral, ethical, and even spiritual, even though they do not believe in God, Christ, or the Church. They are a part of the American landscape, just as Christians are.

Despite all this, the American climate has been generally hospitable to Christianity. The vast majority of Americans believe in God, in Jesus, in the Bible. They want to be thought of as Christian. They welcome churches in their communities. Three out of five of them are members, and two out of five attend regularly. Yet the Church does not have a secure future.

Many of the largely northern churches seem to have grown tired, lost their energies to win new people, and become unsure of their beliefs and purposes. In this sense they look a bit like the old churches of Europe. Their losses have been made up by gains among churches in the Sunbelt, or among fervent Pentecostalists, firm fundamentalists, or exuberant Southern Baptists. But how long before they, too, fall victim to the problems of their time and place?

The American churches have not suffered losses because people believe God has died. They have other problems, related to changes in people's lifestyles. As the nation grows prosperous and people can afford summer homes or sea-and-ski vacations, they are gone weekends, the ordinary times of worship. They vacate the churches. When people live with large families in single-family homes, they take responsibility for their communities. As their children grow, they help the churches educate them. What happens when people move into highrise apartments? They may not feel a part of the community. The Church may be far away, or find it hard to adapt to different lifestyles.

The private way of being religious is another problem. In a Baptist town, a Catholic ward, a Jewish ghetto, or a Mormon state, everything helps accent the importance of faith. The clubs and causes, even the credit unions, were or are part of the religious organization. Sometimes there are parochial schools, or "sectarian" scout troops. One has many supports for the faith. But when "pluralism" rules and there is no community support for one's own faith and one's own church, it is easy to be confused or casual. People believe in Jesus but not the Church, in God but not the Christian community. That is the problem for the churches.

No one expects the churches to have an easy time in the next generation. The mainline Protestant and Catholic churches have to arrest their declines and do more than hold their own. The more aggressive churches, as they move into the mainline, have to work to keep the loyalty of people. Both have to recruit from the stay-at-home population, even as they learn to live in a society whose beliefs do not often match their own.

Despite the odds, however, the church has tremendous assets. Around the world, religion is not dying out; it is only taking different forms, not all of them pleasant. (One thinks of tribal and religious warfare as sad examples: in Lebanon, many African nations, or between Hindus and Muslims in India.) But the presence of religion suggests that modern people do need a sense of the sacred and still discover or devise ways to find it and to express it. In the world, Christianity represents well over a billion people, and in America there are over 100 million faithful. These people gather in hundreds of thousands of places of worship and then disperse into their walks of life.

People are born and initiated into the ancient faith; they train their children and marry before the altars. In the crises of life they turn to religious counselors. For many activities they

find the churches good instruments to help change the world. They try to spread the message by print, radio, television, or, best of all, in person. When they come upon hard times, they know that they still live by the promises of God. They have not been told that they will always be successful. They have no commands that promise constant victories. But they do have the promise that until the end of time, beyond the life of the nations, the power and Spirit of God and the love of Jesus Christ remain with them. For the sake of the world. ●

Index

Christianity in the New World
Christian Churches in the United States

Compiled by Audrey DeLaMartre

Boldface numbers indicate pages in *Christianity in the New World*.
Other numbers indicate pages in *Christian Churches in the United States*.

de Padilla, Juan, **19**
de Santangel, Luis, **13-14**
de Sepulveda, John Gines, **21**
de Soto, Hernando, **24**
Disciples of Christ, 11, 22, 66-68
Dominicans, **122**
Du Bois, W. E. Burghardt, 77
Dunkers. *See* Brethren, Church of
Dutch Reformed Church, **56-57, 76-77,** 22, 56, 81-83
Dyer, Mary, **52-53**

Eastern Orthodox Church, 8, 11, 22, 87-89
Ecumenical, Ecumenism, 17, 30, 68
Eddy, Mary Baker, 9, 97-98. *See also* Church of Christ, Scientist
Education, **22-26, 38,** 55-57, 73-74. *See also* Schools
Edward, Jonathan, **71, 82-85,** 50
Eisenhower, Dwight, 38
Eliot, John, **70-71**
England, English, **32-33, 37, 44-45, 47- 50, 65, 67-73, 100-121, 107-108,** 39, 40, 104
Enlightenment, **72, 94-101, 109,** 117
Episcopal Church, Episcopalians, **32-35, 52, 59, 61, 72, 76-77, 81, 86-87, 100, 106, 108, 119, 124-125,** 11-13, 20, 24, 37, 39-41, 73. *See also* Church of England
Eucharist. *See* Communion, Holy
European Church, 8, 88-89. *See also* Eastern Orthodox, and Roman Catholic Churches.
Evangelical and Reformed Church. *See* United Church of Christ

Federal Council of Churches, 58
Ferdinand, King, **12-14**
Finney, Charles Grandison, 50
Florida, **17, 24-26,** 65, 117
Flushing Remonstrance, **57**
Footwashing, 91
Ford, Gerald, 41
Fox, George, **52**
Franciscans, **18-19, 24-26, 122**
Franklin, Benjamin, **63, 80, 92, 94-95,** 34, 85, 120
Freedom of Religion, **40-41, 44-46, 50-51, 56-59, 98, 109,** 9, 18-19, 56, 82, 97, 101
Freemasonry, **96**
Frelinghuysen, Theodorus, **76-77**
French America, **27, 72-73, 117,** 26-27
Friends, Society of. *See* Quakers
Frontier, **126-127,** 15, 64, 67
Fundamentalism, 37-38, 43, 58, 67-68, 108-109

Gandhi, Mohandas, 49
Georgia, **65-66, 78-79,** 95
German, Germany, **58, 98,** 16, 24, 27, 43, 78, 92

German Reformed Church, 22, 95. *See also* United Church of Christ
Ghost Dance, 114
Gibbons, James Cardinal, 26, 28
Gladden, Washington, 49
"Gospel Visitor," 91
Graham, Billy, 50-51, 64-65
Granada, **12-13**
Greece, Greek, 88-89

Haiti, Haitians, 17
Hakluyt, Richard, **32**
Henry, Patrick, 40
Hindus, Hinduism, 18, 54, 124
Hispanics, 17, 64
Hobart, John Henry, 40
Hodge, Charles, 36-38
Holocaust, 111
Huguenots, **24-29**
Humanism, Humanists, 34-35, 123
Huss, John, 94
Hussites, *See* Moravians
Hutchinson, Anne, **51-52**

Icons, 88
Immigration, Immigrants, **118,** 9, 16-18, 24, 27-28, 111
Inca, 17
Indian, American. *See* Native American
Industrialization, 16
International Bible Students. *See* Jehovah's Witnesses
Iran, 18. *See also* Islam; Muslim
Ireland, Irish, **67-69, 118,** 16, 24, 27- 28, 37
Isabella, **12-14**
Islam, **12-13, 22,** 88-89, 124. *See also* Iran; Muslims
Italians, Italy, 9, 24, 27

Jarratt, Devereaux, **89**
Jefferson, Thomas, **93, 94, 97-98,** 18, 34, 117, 121
Jehovah's Witnesses, 22, 100-101
Jesuits, **24-26, 117, 122**
Jews, **13-14, 32, 41, 112-113,** 10, 13 16, 18, 22, 54, 56, 110-113
Jones, Absalom. *See* Allen, Richard
Jogues, Isaac, **28**
John XXIII, Pope, 29
Judson, Adoniram, 53

Kansas, **19**
Kellogg family, 97
King, Martin Luther, Jr., 49, 72, 74
King's Chapel, 35
Kino, Eusebino, **19**
Knights of Labor, 28
Kurtz, Henry, 91

Labor, 28
Labor Unions, 26, 48-49
Laity: responsibility of, 18, 32-33; participation of, 30; power of, **117,** 32
Latter-Day Saints, Church of, 9, 11-13, 22, 69-71. *See also* Smith, Joseph
Liberia (Africa), 77. *See also* Colonization
Lincoln, Abraham, 121
Locke, John, **100**
Lord's Supper. *See* Communion, Holy
Loyalists, **106, 108, 118,** 40. *See also* Church of England; Episcopal
Luther, Martin, 78
Lutheran Church, Lutherans, **58-64, 66, 99, 124-125,** 9-10, 12-13, 22, 56

Machen, John Gresham, 108-109
Madison, James, **94, 108,** 18, 40
Makemie, Francis, **68-69**
Maryland, **40-41, 72, 117-118,** 27
Mason, George, 40
Massachusetts, **48, 51,** 82
Massachusetts Bay Colony, **47-50**
Mather, Cotton, **113**
Mayhew, Jonathan, **100-101**
Mennonites, **61, 106,** 23, 92-93
Methodist Church, Methodists, **78-79, 88- 89, 114-116,** 9-10, 12, 15, 22, 35, 37, 60-62, 73, 102-104; black, 22, 75-77
Mexican, Mexico, **17-19, 122**
Millennial Dawnists. *See* Jehovah's Witnesses
Miller, William, 97
Missionaries, Missions, **18-29, 33, 40-41, 70, 126-127,** 15, 40, 48, 52-54, 70, 74, 88, 95
Monroe, James, 41
Moody, Dwight L. 50-51, 54
Moors. *See* Islam; Muslims
Moral issues: abortion, 108; alcohol, 47-49, 63, 97; diet, 97: environment, 49; homosexuality, 108; integration, 51; nuclear disarmament, 49, 120; outreach, 27, 46-48; pacifism, **106,** 91, 93, 95; poverty, 47, 49, 102; pornography, 108; service, 91, 93, 102-104; slavery, **16- 23, 27, 33, 38, 92-93,** 15, 35, 37, 47-48, 50, 65, 73, 90-91, 121; war, 49, 90-91
Moravians, **62, 66, 79,** 8, 22, 94-95
Mormons. *See* Latter-Day Saints, Church of; Smith, Joseph
Mott, John R. 53-54
Muhlenberg, Henry, 63-64, 106
Muslims, **12-13, 32,** 54, 124. *See also* Iran; Islam

National Association of Evangelicals, 59
National Cathedral, 41
National Council of Churches, 58, 91
Nationalism. *See* Civil Religion
Native Americans, Native American Church, **15-33, 36-38, 45, 62, 70-71, 113, 121-122,** 16, 22, 40, 52, 69, 95, 114-115
Negro. *See* Blacks
Netherlands, 82
Nevin, John Williamson, 86